THE ART OF FASHION
ILLUSTRATION

First published in the United States of America by
Rockport Publishers, a member of
Quarto Publishing Group USA Inc.
100 Cummings Center
Suite 406-L
Beverly, Massachusetts 01915-6101
Telephone: (978) 282-9590
Fax: (978) 283-2742
www.rockpub.com

Library of Congress Cataloging-in-Publication Data available

ISBN: 978-1-63159-013-9

Digital edition published in 2015

eISBN: 978-1-63159-013-9

10 9 8 7 6 5 4 3 2 1

Cover and Book designed by Laia Albaladejo
Cover Image: *Blueberry*, Pippa McManus
Illustrations on pages 140; 142–144; back flap, by Julia Kuo.

Printed in China

Somer Flaherty Tejwani

THE ART OF FASHION ILLUSTRATION

Learn the techniques and inspiration of today's leading fashion artists

Rockport Publishers
100 Cummings Center, Suite 406L
Beverly, MA 01915

rockpub.com • rockpaperink.com

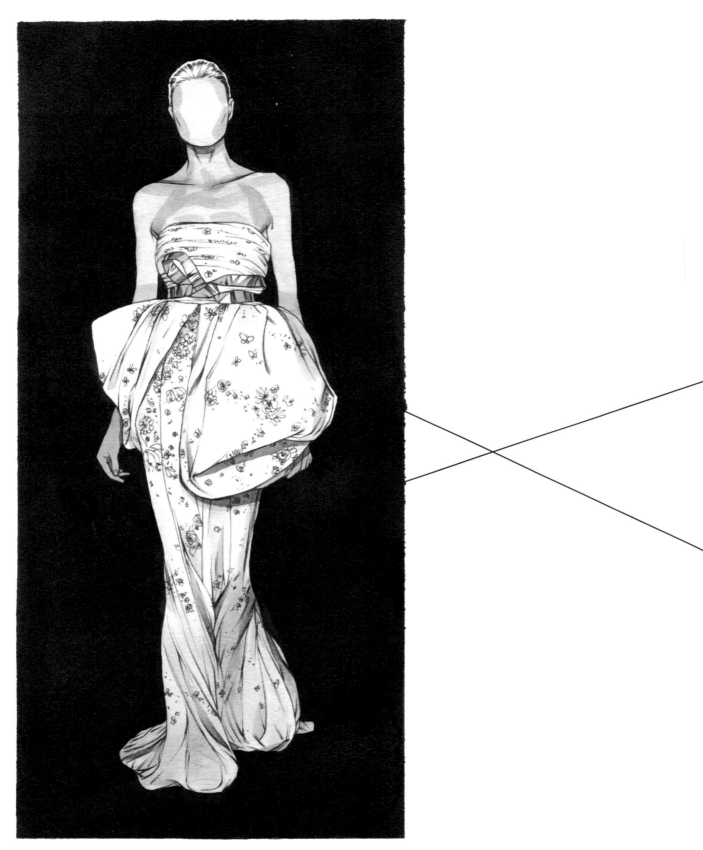

Look 35, a runway study of a look from Giambattista Valli, by Michael Hoeweler.

CONTENTS

Part 1: The Emerging Masters

Part 2: The Icons

Fashion illustrations allow the design fantasy to come to life. It is a road map to new ideas; and one sketch can often spiral, cultivating a unique emotional connection, influencing an entire collection.

—**Fashion Designer, CFDA/Vogue Fashion Fund Finalist Misha Nonoo of Nonoo New York**

Kitty N. Wong's Bunny
A fashion illustration painted with acrylic on recycled cardboard, inspired by the runway collection of Undercover by Jun Takahashi.

INTRODUCTION TO FASHION ILLUSTRATION

A fashion illustration does something that a photograph can never do: It provides a direct connection to the designer and brings the energy and style within the clothing to reality. The illustrator's job is to find the balance between the drawing as a whole and the details in it that bring the garment to life.

Fashion illustration provides the rare opportunity to savor a moment in history, long after the relevance of the clothing itself. *The Art of Fashion Illustration* includes interviews and illustrations from those who have seized this opportunity: both the emerging masters—the illustration world's next big names—and the icons, a group whose body of work has already made their names recognizable.

What's surprising is that many of the featured artists didn't find their "fashion" calling until it was presented to them as an option in college. With hindsight they wonder if they should have seen the signs all along—the moments as a kid when they would tear the advertisements out of fashion magazines or collect beautiful images of models.

Although their paths to becoming illustrators may have been different, one of the most refreshing characteristics of all the artists interviewed is that style is a signature dwelling. Some rely on traditional techniques such as pen and paper to realize their images, while others prefer to use digital options. Some love infusing rich and bold color, and others prefer to create in black and white. But the common shared experience among all the artists is that illustration is a career where diligence and perseverance pays off, and one in which the artists should never underestimate their ability to draw.

Editorial illustration for Danish fashion magazine, *Eurowoman*, by Wendy Plovmand.

"A good fashion illustration should not only capture the vision of the designer, it should drive the essence of the times."

—Simon Ungless, Director of the School of Fashion at Academy of Art University

PART 1
THE EMERGING MASTERS

DEVELOPING HER OWN VISUAL LANGUAGE: ZOË TAYLOR

London, England

> **Fashion illustration has somehow become this distinct category, but I just see it as another form of illustration.**

Zoë Taylor's work has appeared in various publications including the *New Guardian*, the *Independent*, *Dazed and Confused*, and *Le Gun*. She has been commissioned to design a series of images to be printed on T-shirts, tote bags, and dresses for the Marc Jacobs fashion line, and has collaborated on a number of projects with fashion designer Luella Bartley.

Zoë Taylor finds it difficult to describe her technique. "It eventually emerges instinctively for everyone if you do enough drawing," she says. Taylor's work can be identified by her frequent use of pastels—she prefers chalky ones such as charcoal and uses them to create contrast, incorporating the duality of very light strokes and stronger lines throughout an image—and by her detailed background drawings. These two characteristics are not often seen in fashion illustration. Unlike other illustrators who create their fashion silhouettes on a blank background, Taylor's work always sets a scene. She attributes this to the fact that she didn't train as a fashion illustrator. Her illustrations have a sense of drama and narrative and capture a scene the way fashion photographs do. The setting suggests something beyond the clothing, and the models in her illustrations become characters. "I sketch out the whole composition and then focus on the person's face, building the elements of the drawing together—a mark on the dress here, a shadow on the tree there—like a painter, I guess."

Pastels An illustration of a Louis Vuitton SS12 outfit for an article in the column "In the Cut" for Anothermag.com.

Taylor's home studio space, where she often works late into the night.

"I draw full scenes and the drawings are tonal so the effect is a bit like looking at photos or film stills."

She says the hardest part is to make the drawings look spontaneous after all the planning and the stress of a deadline. "I sometimes draw things thirty times over to try to get it right, and I usually start with the eyes." She believes spontaneity is important in an illustration because if you can see where an artist has struggled or labored with a drawing it brings attention to that and takes away from the overall effect of the image.

Over the years Taylor's work has evolved to include more color, and often the clothing dictates her color choices—although she likes using very bright, intense colors in small patches. "When I'm constructing scenes, I think about the colors I want in the background and how that would contrast with and complement the colors of the clothes; occasionally that's given me ideas about the kind of landscape or interior I choose for the illustration."

Good Advice

"Fashion illustration has somehow become this distinct category, but I just see it as another form of illustration. I'd like to see more narrative in fashion drawing. Stylists and photographers have so much fun hinting at characters and stories through fashion spreads, and anything is possible with drawing—you don't have to worry about the budget and you can cast whoever you want."

Taylor recalls the advice she was given by her tutor, artist Andrzej Klimowski, who passed it down from his tutor, famed poster designer Henryk Tomaszewski. "Klimowski used to say 'personal work is professional hygiene.' If you don't keep making your own work along with your commissions, your professional work becomes dull. That's very true." Taylor believes it's important to look, read, and watch as much as possible. "You don't need to worry about fitting in with styles that are already out there—focus instead on developing your own visual language."

Tweed A Zoë Taylor pastel on newsprint, an illustration of a Prada SS12 outfit for an article about floral appliqués in the column "In the Cut" for Anothermag.com.

PERSISTENCE IS KEY TO SUCCESS: MASHA KARPUSHINA

London, England

Have a dream. Find the steps to get to that dream and make it happen. I think this pretty much sums up the way I try to lead my life now.

Masha Karpushina works from home at a desk with "heaps of material all around it" in a corner of her living room dedicated to her work. A scene she says is not a pretty sight, but functional. It is here that she starts sketching. If she is creating work for a client, she will send the sketch for approval and once it is approved, she will redraw that same image by tracing the outlines of the image onto a better quality paper using a light box, and then add more details and make any small corrections. All corrections happen at the sketch stage, and once it is final she will scan the image, clean it up digitally, and send it to the client.

London's Masha Karpushina proves that opportunity comes in many forms. Her first illustration job was for Duncan McNamara at East London's streetwear fashion brand, Illustrated People. The job with Duncan started by coincidence. "At the time, I was working for a trendy French–Brazilian-owned club called Favela Chic in Shoreditch. For their first New Year's Eve party they wanted an extravagant invitation printed on a pair of knickers," recalls Karpushina. "In Brazil, it's considered good luck for the year to wear a new pair of underwear on New Year's Eve." She worked with McNamara on the invitation, and he offered her a job. She designed her first T-shirts for Illustrated People. "It was easy, fun, and really rewarding. There was no pressure, and the briefs were really loose, so essentially we could draw whatever we wanted. A dream job," she says.

LA meets Cyber Beauty
The client wanted palm trees
in the image because they
were part of the inspiration
for the collection. "Palm trees
for me mean Los Angeles,—
the city I have been visiting
on and off for the past twenty
years. I wanted the illustration to feel surreal, abstract,
and beautiful at the same
time," says Karpushina.
Mashakarpushina.com.

August "[This piece] was about the world of the real and surreal, the waking state and the sleep, our dreams, and realities. I used my two-year-old son's drawings as part of the collage to give it some young and pure energy," Karpushina says. Mashakarpushina.com.

Good Advice

Like most beginning freelancers, Karpushina says her biggest challenge was finding clients and knowing what to charge them. "Then I got an agent and learned, bit by bit, how to charge and the rates one can expect," she adds. For illustrators who are just starting out, she says patience and persistence are key to succeeding, along with learning how to market yourself and your work. She says her best advice comes from her dad. "Have a dream. Find the steps to get to that dream, and make it happen. I think this pretty much sums up the way I try to lead my life now."

Although she's had great success with illustration, working with brands such as All Saints, Armada Skis, and Illustrated People, Karpushina has also taken time away from drawing. "My youngest son is just over two. Children change something. They make you really appreciate time so you work differently."

Meadow Print for Mrs Pomeranz Dress "Mrs Pomeranz is a company owned by a friend of mine, Dasha, who asked me to draw this print for a summer dress they had in mind," says Masha Karpushina. Mashakarpushina.com.

Delirium Jacket "Armada Skis asked me to draw a black and white print for their skis. It was a success so we extended the same print to fit a jacket," Karpushina says. "The print itself is a combination of previously drawn artworks; it's a kaleidoscope of emotions." Mashakarpushina.com.

CREATIVE INTERPRETATION: ADRIANA KRAWCEWICZ

London, England

Draw, observe, and experiment.

Adriana Krawcewicz says her style is constantly evolving and she finds it exciting to allow herself to change as an artist. She describes her technique as a graphic playground of constructivism. Starting out as an illustrator she experimented with media, technique, and approach—a time she calls a roller coaster ride. Her work is known for its juxtaposition of color and graphic elements. Although she feels more comfortable working in black and white, color brings out a dramatic effect in her pieces.

Poland-born and London-based illustrator Adriana Krawcewicz feels fashion illustration is making a comeback. Unlike photography, she says an illustration has no limitations and therefore unending creative opportunities.

She has also found that fashion illustration can go beyond a commercial, beauty image—she says it can be applied to many other creative fields such as fashion films, editorials, and set design. This expanded vision has led to successes including creating murals for the fortieth anniversary exhibition of makeup brand Cosmetics à La Carte in London, having an illustration retweeted by Chanel on Twitter, and starting a personal fashion blog of street-style illustration called Line Hunter.

Illustration by Adriana Krawcewicz

Influences

When Krawcewicz was eighteen years old and living in the United States she was greatly inspired by the U.S. fashion magazines. "They really appealed to my sense of creativity and made me look at illustration from a fashionable point of view," she says. She's not a fan of realistic illustrations of models in garments. "I personally find them boring and lacking depth." For her, a fashion illustrator's role is to use creative interpretation and to leave realism to the photographers. The need to interpret fashion illustration in her own way was a process of exploring that took years. In the beginning she says it was hard to pin down what the genre was really all about—is it a portrait or is it an illustration of a garment? But she experimented with media and technique and found her voice.

Like many other fashion illustrators Krawcewicz has been influenced by René Gruau, whom she calls "the pioneer of fashion illustration," and designers John Galliano and Mary Katrantzou, and illustrator Antonio Lopez.

Good Advice

"Draw, observe, and experiment. I think technique and solid skills are the key to developing a signature style, and I truly believe in the power of experience."

Illustrations by Adriana Krawcewicz.

NEVER GIVING UP:
SARAH BEETSON

Queensland, Australia

Keep moving forward.

While at art school Sarah Beetson was initially using a number of techniques to create her work, none of which she was in love with. During life-drawing classes, students were taught the blind contour drawing technique, in which the artist places the pen or pencil on the paper and looks at the subject, drawing "blindly" without taking his or her eyes from the subject. "This technique can be totally haphazard with moments of clarity, a mess of abstract lines with a perfect hand or eye within it," she says. "I decided to combine this technique with a number of other materials and styles I liked to work with, and hence my style was born."

Beetson begins an illustration by creating a background. She works on paper, wood, photographic prints, or fabric and often uses spray paint, tissue paper, or collage techniques for the background. She creates the line work of the piece using Pilot G Tec C pens. "The rest is a combination of an exhaustive list of materials which I am constantly adding to, but often includes acrylic gouache, markers, gel pens, crayon, stickers, vintage magazine clippings, beads, and sequins."

Unlike some illustrators who prefer black and white, Beetson is drawn to color and says it is the most fundamentally important element that drives her to create illustrations. She favors bright hues, pastels, and neon colors.

Erdem "This piece was commissioned by The British Fashion Council to promote their Fashion Forward award. Nominees for the award that year were Erdem, Roksanda Ilincic, Christopher Kane, and Marios Schwab. I got to choose one look from each of their collections to illustrate," says Sarah Beetson, who used a variety of media including pen, spray paint, acrylic gouache, markers, crayons, and stickers.

Exotically Moleskin paper, pen, spray paint, acrylic gouache, stickers, postage stamps. "This piece is from a series of personal work that celebrates the work of John Galliano at Dior."

Starting out as a fashion illustrator wasn't easy for Sarah Beetson. After receiving an illustration degree she found herself living in London and struggling to climb the creative ladder. "The term 'impoverished artist' is an understatement," she says, recalling how she existed on little money, which she cobbled together from numerous bar jobs while interning in the fashion industry full time and paying rent in London's pricy housing market. "I relied on tips to cover bus fare to work and I fed myself by eating whatever free food was offered at my job. I literally ate one decent meal a day."

At one point she considered leaving London until bartending friends who were using London's abandoned buildings to live in and as studio space let her squat for a short time. She saved enough money to rent a new flat and take on a job that began as a one-day-a-week portfolio assistant and blossomed into an international role as a talent scout for an illustration agency. She still works at the agency today and is responsible for reviewing thousands of submissions from artists.

Floral Boots "This piece was created for a series of greeting cards based on shoes. The boots were inspired by my own vintage 'bouquet noir' Doc Martens from 1991," says Beetson of her mixed media illustration.

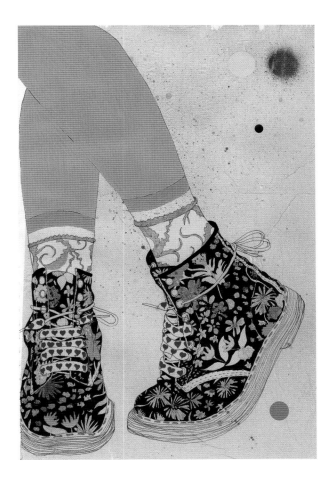

EXUBERANTLY

Influences

"I met some amazing creative people in those squats, who are now successful actors, burlesque stars, artists, fashion designers, and TV tarot sensations!" says Beetson. It was during this time that she developed her portfolio, and found illustration agents in Canada and in London. "It was so hard at the time, but I'm glad I went through it as it makes me so thankful for where I am today. It was worth it for the career I was able to develop," she says.

Beetson worked with Stella McCartney in the early days of her label, where she learned the value of research in shaping the foundations of any creative project. She created large-scale paintings and illustrations for a fashion marketing company with top name clients and has illustrated for major newspapers including the *Globe and Mail* (Toronto), the *Times* (UK), the *Telegraph* (UK), and the *Miami Herald*. She has won the Creative Review (UK) Best in Book prize for illustration in 2011, and was invited to exhibit the best from the last five years of her work at an exhibit in Paris called "Rainbowspective."

Beetson has been influenced by designers and artists in various design fields: Spanish architect Antoni Gaudi, Austrian painters Gustav Klimt and Egon Schiele, artist Julie Verhoeven, famed illustrator Antonio Lopez, writer and artist Henry Darger, Japanese painter and sculptor Yoshitomo Nara, and film director John Waters.

Good Advice

"In the beginning, take on every job you're offered to elevate your position as an illustrator and raise your profile. Keep developing your work and strive forward even if you are having trouble breaking into the industry. Approach the clients you want to work for. Find innovative ways to present your work. But above all, keep creating it, follow advice when you receive it, and keep moving forward."

A DIFFERENT PATH:
AUDRIA BRUMBERG

Los Angeles, California

**Develop good aesthetic and a good
eye for what truly is good work.**

It can take up to a week for artist Audria Brumberg to complete an illustration. Her work is identifiable by her unique style, which includes both realistic model figures, based on images of friends or old photo shoots, and abstract patterns, based on sketching items in nature.

With an arsenal of materials that include pen, paper, scanner, light box, and her computer, she starts her illustrations with a sketch that she then scans in to her computer to digitally manipulate. She will draw every piece of the illustration separately and then vector out anything abstract because creating a vector image will allow her to scale the individual pieces of the drawing so none becomes blurry or pixilated. She considers this piece-by-piece procedure, with all the pieces coming together to create the final work of art, the fun part of the illustration process.

Audria Brumberg began her path to illustration via graphic design. She never thought about illustration as a career but as she became active in the graphic design community in New York, clients began to notice her illustrations.

Electric Brumberg notes, "This piece was inspired by New Wave music and the early '90s—using solid lines and bright colors in the background really makes the woman pop."

Influences

Brumberg came to New York from the west coast during the recession, which made finding work difficult at first. It took good, old-fashioned networking including meeting other designers and artists, getting referrals, and sending lots of emails to break through at a time when artist commissions and freelance projects were drying up.

Her style is organic and photo-driven and with what she calls an art nouveau feeling. Brumberg's work has a very signature look—and can often be recognized by how she illustrates the subject's hair, which is dripping in texture, a style she developed when she was a child and continues to use in all her work. Her unique style has led to commissioned illustrations for a Berlin department store and a fashion lookbook, as well as art direction for popular fashion brands and websites.

Brumberg finds inspiration in architecture, product design, and '70s punk album covers. She takes a minimalist approach to her graphic design work following the work of Japanese designer and curator Kenya Hara and German industrial designer Dieter Rams. "When I do illustrations I throw all the rules out. It's like I have a split personality when it comes to my work."

Good Advice

Constantly look at what other designers are doing and develop good taste, says Brumberg. Follow design blogs and study the campaigns created by fashion designers to develop a good aesthetic and an eye for good work. Expose yourself to more and more good work. But she cautions that it's important to stay true to your own style and develop your voice because that is what people will hire you for.

A

B

C

D

E

A.
Suduction [sic] "I really love the '20s and Art Deco. This illustration embodies a modern-day flapper," says Brumberg.

B.
New Wave "This piece was inspired by shapes and the exploration of textures."

C.
Wonder Mixed media with ink, pen, Illustrator, Photoshop, and Photography by Audria Brumberg.

D.
Peach "This started as a sketch that then I incorporated the model. I love how she's intertwined with the lines around her," Brumberg says.

E.
An illustration for a lookbook. Brumberg notes, "I kept the model black and white to bring attention to the clothing."

AN ALWAYS-EVOLVING STYLE: KITTY N. WONG

Hong Kong

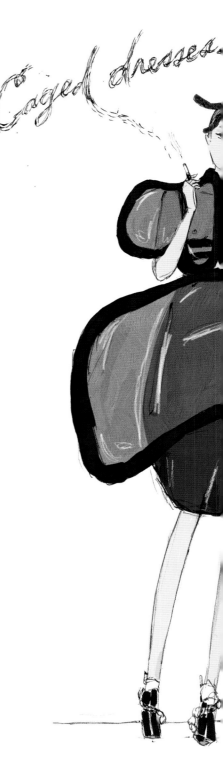

Caged dresses

For illustration, the barrier to entry is set much lower than something like starting your own fashion line. You just need your sketches, time, and some social skills, and you can be on your way to getting clients.

Hong Kong–based illustrator Kitty N. Wong starts her illustrations with what she calls a very rough draft but proceeds to the final version quickly, otherwise she feels the spontaneity is lost and the energy can never be captured again. Although her style is always evolving—and she likes to experiment with different techniques—there are two constants in her work: Her images tell a story and the lines she creates are smooth, fluid, and relaxed. As Wong's confidence in illustration evolved, so did her work and the result is an infusion of color and patterns. She counts humor as part of her style—something she says is rare for a fashion illustrator—and the evidence is the witty fashion comic strips she has been commissioned to create.

Perhaps one of the most promising new illustrators in the field is Kitty N. Wong. Still only in her twenties, the Hong Kong–based artist, who grew up in Canada, has already made a splash creating custom sketches depicting designer runway looks for a top fashion blog, as well as published pieces for the *Hong Kong Tatler*, *Dazed Digital*, and the *National Post* in Canada.

Comme des Garçons A fashion comic created in ballpoint pen and colored digitally, from a series for Dazed Digital Halloween, "If Fashion Week was a Horror Film" featuring Comme des Garçons, SS14's darkest collection.

Influences

Wong's soft and ethereal, yet realistic illustration style was cultivated through years of practice. She's been drawing since she was a child and would spend time in high school researching fashion online. "Looking up runway photos and sketching my ideas was my hobby. It was the most accessible way for me to participate in the fashion world as a young girl living in a small Canadian suburb," says Wong. Although she took fashion illustration classes at Toronto's Ryerson University and completed an undergraduate degree in fashion design, she says she doesn't believe a person can be formally trained in fashion illustration, and says most of the important things she has learned have been by drawing and by observing other artist's work.

After graduation, Wong honed her skills working as an assistant designer drawing fashion sketches and technical drawings for a trading company. But the real turning point happened when she quit her job and started to freelance.

"My favorite parts about working from home are my commute and the huge long desk my dad and I built—it's big enough so I can separate my work spaces," Wong says. "I have a painting side for all the messy analog processes and a computer side where I clean up the images and write."

"Starting out as a freelance illustrator was intimidating, and I felt like I had no idea what I was doing, but I met some good people who gave me a few jobs either for trade or for small amounts of money. I was able to get started and build my confidence and skills," she says. "For illustration, the barrier to entry is set much lower than for something like starting your own fashion line. You just need your sketches, time, and some social skills, and you can be on your way to getting clients."

Maison Martin Margiela A fashion comic created in ballpoint pen and colored digitally, for Dazed Digital Halloween, "If Fashion Week was a Horror Film."

Every few days Wong finishes a new piece, and although she says it doesn't feel like much, over time she's been able to build up her portfolio. "When I was working for someone else, I neglected my own practice and, at the end of the day, I had nothing I was truly proud of to show for my time. I really treasure this ability to make art. I could have easily gone through life without realizing what kind of work I was passionate about."

Wong feeds her need to draw by keeping random pieces of scrap paper in her purse so she can make a quick sketch and a notebook next to her bed to jot down ideas in the middle of the night. She also says it's important to see a lot of art and make a lot of art. In Hong Kong she has done just that, visiting what she calls "phenomenal private art galleries." Her influences are varied, and include everything from vintage items from the 1950s to the works of influential designers and artists such as graphic designer Louise Fili, famed fashion illustrator René Gruau, and painter Henri Matisse.

Good Advice

Looking back on her career so far, Wong says the biggest challenge was feeling unsure of herself and being intimidated. "I thought there were all these rules I had to follow. There are no rules except the ones you set for yourself."

"A Kate Moss portrait in progress, part of the Women I've Wanted to Be series," says Kitty N. Wong. The artwork is surrounded by the artist's gouache palette, paint test strips, and a fashion illustration postcard from her Etsy shop.

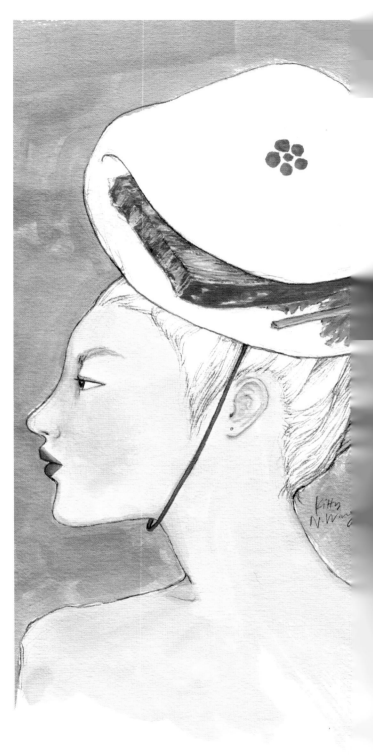

Madame Bao An editorial illustration merging food and fashion created for the January 2014 issue of the *Hong Kong Tatler* for a story about the city's hottest food trend: the steamed bao.

BORN TO ILLUSTRATE:
SARAH HANKINSON

Melbourne, Australia

> **I treated each illustration job as a path to gain exposure and therefore more work.**

Sarah Hankinson's technique uses a combination of traditional drawing and mixed media, and she is known for her distinct line work—she likes to use strong and confident lines that vary in thickness to add contrast, interest, and strength to her illustrations. "The use of a beautiful line can make an illustration," she says.

Her work stands out with the bold splashes of watercolor she incorporates. "I love watercolors and the expressive nature of the medium. I tend to not think too much about which colors to use. I just go with what feels right!"

She begins her illustrations by using a "dangerously sharp 2B gray lead pencil" to draw the model on soft watercolor paper. Hankinson prefers this type of paper because it accepts water well, not crinkling too much. "I use a smooth paper so my line work isn't fuzzy and the pencil glides more easily across the paper." She then brings in color to add interest to the piece. "After scanning the image I play around with the curves and layers in Photoshop to adjust the contrast." In art school one of the first things Hankinson learned was how to use contrast to her advantage. She says contrast can create a strong, clear focal point in a piece and can make a flat image pop. She adjusts the levels in her scanned piece in Photoshop to create just the right contrast and make the piece look more visually appealing. "I try to make each piece a balance of light and dark, thick and thin lines, empty and full space."

Meet Me at the Flatiron "The Flatiron is one of my favorite New York buildings; it's just so cool! I love that it's right near Madison Square Park and Eataly—such a good spot to stock up on delicious Italian produce," says Sarah Hankinson of her pencil and watercolor illustration.

Boom Boom Room "This illustration was inspired by my trip to New York and getting ready for the perfect night out," the artist notes. "Gypsy Water is my favorite perfume, and I love having a cocktail while I'm getting ready. The Boom Boom Room is a bar at The Standard High Line, a hotel in the Meatpacking District; it has amazing views of New York City and is the perfect venue for a night on the town."

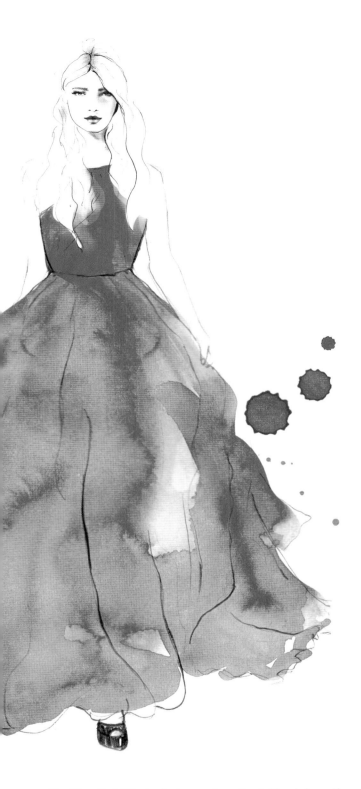

Illustrator Sarah Hankinson grew up with a dressmaker for a mom, so she was always around fabrics and clothing, and while studying she worked part-time in fashion stores to feed her love for the industry. "I love fashion and I follow many models so it was natural for me to draw these images and take my career on this path," she says. "I feel like I never really made this choice, I just fell into it. I have been drawing for as long as I remember." She likes the intimacy of fashion illustration. "It can express a look or feel instantly."

Influences

Hankinson spent a lot of the early days sending drawing samples to potential clients. "I treated each illustration job as a path to gain exposure and therefore more work," she says. Her tenacity paid off with clients ranging from *Harper's Bazaar* to Maybelline New York–Australia, and a commission from Target USA to create an illustration profile for its Facebook page. "Each month they have a different illustrator from around the world create a profile, and it was such an honor to be featured alongside such amazing illustrators as Kathryn Elyse Rodgers and Stina Persson, who have inspired me greatly, particularly when I was starting out."

Good Advice

Starting out in the field was daunting for Hankinson. Although it can take a while to reach success, she says if you have the motivation to push and market yourself work will come.

She Wore Red "The inspiration was Australian fashion designer Alex Perry. I loved the dress, the color, and movement—it's just so beautiful and was really fun to illustrate," Hankinson explains.

IMMERSED IN THE WORLD OF FASHION: PIPPA MCMANUS

Perth, Australia

> **One of the best things I learned while studying was mistakes lead to great things!**

Pippa McManus creates illustrations that stay etched in your memory long after you've looked at the beautiful images. Her well-known works include illustrations of women on a monochromatic acrylic background with the focus on the woman's hair and eyes. She always includes flowers somewhere in the piece. When she creates an illustration she goes through what she calls her mental rolodex of past fashion editorials and fashion shows, choosing various reference images from pieces that she loves—the face from one image, the pose or hair from another. When creating a commissioned piece she makes a small pencil sketch based on her reference or assigned subject and then describes the composition and style so that the client can see how the end product will look. If she is painting or drawing for herself, she'll just start creating on her canvas. "I was taught in art class in primary school never to use an eraser, so that means I have to work [the illustration] out thoroughly first or let my mistakes become part of the piece."

Pippa McManus has been illustrating professionally for more than a decade. She studied fine art, fashion, and textile design at the Western Australian School of Art Design & Media. In addition to attending fashion week shows in Sydney, where she sketches the fashions as they come down the runway, her work has been featured in magazines, exhibited in galleries, and even replicated on fashionable tote bags.

Gemma for Prada
"One of my favorite models is Gemma Ward, and I painted this just after I met her at a friend's thirtieth birthday party in our mutual hometown of Perth, Western Australia. It was quite embarrassing: I was completely starstruck and hardly remember anything about the encounter (possibly also due to a little too much Champagne!). So I knew I had to do her justice and redeem myself when I painted her the next week. The original picture is from a Prada advertisement; this was also my first experiment using white spray paint rather than only black," says McManus.

Marcelina in Mustard "I was coming up with ideas for my next exhibition, and kept bookmarking images of girls reclining, half asleep and half awake, and in soft relaxed poses as opposed to 'the high fashion, right angles, and hard expressions' look that I had been painting at that time," McManus says. "I also wanted to start painting patterns, or more specifically painting painted textile patterns, a replica of a replica of a replica! The piece flowed so easily as I painted her; she was the first for the exhibition, which I always think is a predictor for the way the rest of the work will get executed. I decided to give her bright red lips so they would pop out from the mustardy color palette."

Byzantine Barbara "I was quite obsessed with model Barbara Palvin at the time I did this. She was just starting to get some big contracts like Victoria's Secret and L'Oreal where she was portrayed in quite an overly sexy and seductive way, so I wanted to do an 'innocent Barbara.' The client forwarded me some beaded and embellished gowns and jewelry that she liked, so I chose what I liked from her selection and 'dressed' Barbara. I used metallic paint pens for the complicated jewelry. Unlike a loaded brush they don't run out as frequently," says McManus.

Influences

When McManus started her career, her work included very photorealistic illustrations, which were in lead pencil. "But I always had my fine art lecturer's voice in the back of my head saying 'Cameras are here for photorealism, artists are here to interpret what is in front of them.' So I focused on elongation, warping, and enlargement and reduction of features. I also spent a year forcing myself to work color into my pieces and I have never looked back."

McManus says the use of color in her work reflects the way she dresses. "I'm rarely seen in black and I have a full-blown obsession with patterned and brightly-colored clothing, so color for me is a necessity," she says. "When it comes to the colorless body, face, and hair in my work, I'm not sure why that is. When I was in art school, I spent all my time replicating skin color in oils and felt like I got as far as I could with it, but now I would love to explore it more."

Good Advice

McManus tries not to refer to other illustrators' work for inspiration, because she doesn't want to be influenced by them. "I absorb things I see quickly and sometimes subconsciously. So if I only look at designer's creations and models, I'm much more likely to turn that into something of my own rather than draw from other illustrators' techniques and styles," McManus says.

Blueberry "The piece was 1200 x 1500 mm (47 x 59 inches), so it's huge!" explains Pippa McManus. "I got to be quite free with the acrylic paint and make the most of the paint running down the canvas at a fast rate, using spray bottles filled with water and sponges to drag sections."

Feathers

"I came across a great shoot of a girl wearing a feather headdress, which I had never drawn before. I love a bit of a 'shoulder up' girl because it's coy and innocent, but sexy at the same time (especially when there are freckles involved). In the shot, the girl had flecks of gold across her cheeks so I thought this was the perfect time to experiment with gold leaf. I'd never used it before and didn't bother doing a trial run first. One of the best things I learned while studying was mistakes lead to great things! It did take a while to get the hang of working with gold leaf because I couldn't get a solid piece down but in the end it worked out perfectly," says McManus.

Veronica in Lace

"This is probably one of the sexiest pieces I have done! At the time I was shopping for lingerie to wear under my wedding dress and could not find a single thing I liked anywhere. I searched the Internet, I went on a trip to Hong Kong, trawled every little bespoke lingerie label I found on Instagram, and still nothing!" McManus explains. "So I think I had underwear on the brain, and when I'm obsessing over something it comes out consciously or subconsciously in my work. I made up this bralette from everything I had taken in over my underwear search, and it left me wondering why couldn't the things I conjure up just appear out of thin air the way they do when I paint them? This is the first background I had ever done that wasn't a flat solid color, and the feedback on it was awesome," says McManus.

THE WIDE VIEW: WENDY PLOVMAND

Copenhagen, Denmark

> **Today the borders between the creative fields are eliminated, creating a bigger audience and many more possibilities for your work.**

Wendy Plovmand uses a technique that she describes as a mix of hand-drawn elements, which she creates using pen, pencil, and watercolor, and then scans to digitally manipulate in Photoshop. Her work begins by researching words and images that she'll use as reference or inspiration for the piece. She works in layers, adding detail upon detail to create what she describes as a collage technique. Something unique to her style: She will often incorporate one piece from a previous work in a current work—creating a symbiotic relationship between her art pieces and manifesting a kind of family hierarchy.

She likes it when fashion illustration merges with other art styles and techniques—inventing something new—which could be why her illustrations don't follow any specific rules regarding movement or texture. She uses a lot of black and white in her work but likes to discover new color combinations that surprise her, and enjoys working with certain color palettes such as pastel colors in one work or almost monochrome colors in another work.

Sonia by Sonia Rykiel

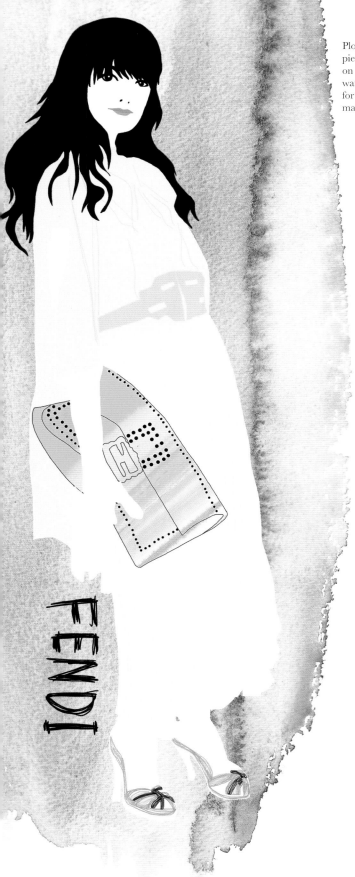

Plovmand created this piece in Photoshop on a hand-drawn watercolor background for Danish fashion magazine *Eurowoman*.

FENDI

Wendy Plovmand illustration for *Eurowoman*.

Influences

Although she describes her signature style as "supernatural fairy tale meets pop meets nature, with a hint of darkness," Plovmand has been inspired by some of the leading artists in the pop art movement including Andy Warhol and Keiichi Tanaami and she admires younger illustrators like Klaus Haapaniemi and Kustaa Saksi.

"The collage was layered beneath the pencil drawing of the women," says Plovmand of this editorial illustration for *Eurowoman*.

Good Advice

Plovmand says you need to have a brave and stubborn soul to achieve success in life as an artist. "As an artist and illustrator you will always feel challenged," says Plovmand. "Lots of times artists have had economical challenges but somehow with will and good ideas and stubbornness we have managed. And even now I sometimes have a month where I think, 'Hmmm, it would be nice to have a paid job now,' and then everything turns around, and suddenly I need to decline projects because I'm too busy."

She takes a wider view on what fashion illustration encompasses, saying it can be art, graphic design, communication, textile design, and interior designer. "Today the borders between the creative fields are eliminated creating a bigger audience and many more possibilities for your work. There is no limit for what you could do with it!"

CREATING HER OWN PATH: SILJA GÖTZ

Madrid, Spain

Try to apply your style to as many subjects as possible. That way you'll learn more and keep your work interesting for you and others.

Silja Götz has three different major styles or techniques. The first she describes as a mix of drawing and collage, where she works with different pens, brushes, and various papers; the second uses a combination of black silhouettes with intricate black and white drawing; and the third is a colorful swirling line drawings she creates in Photoshop. Even with these variations, Götz says she is always adapting to the client and the subject so it's hard to maintain one recognizable style. "Still my work is very personal and something of me always seeps into the outcome."

Editorial commissions usually start with a short description of the text her image will accompany along with the approximate size needed. "I generally have a solution right away, which may not always be the best one, but it gives me a starting point. I toy around with this idea, look for material online, and start drawing different elements. As the illustration is taking form, some things are discarded, others added, and everything is scanned and colored or rearranged in Photoshop. It's quite a lot of back and forth between the drawing desk and the computer," she says.

Pandora's Box "For the dress, I was toying with different bits of paper I had lying around," notes artist Silja Götz.

Silja Götz's start in the field of fashion illustration was surprisingly simple. "It happened to coincide with a very propitious moment for illustration in magazines and advertising," she says. "Illustrations had been all but forgotten for many years, but in the late 1990s people suddenly thought they were fresh and exciting again." She sent out a self-published illustrated book to potential clients, and showed her portfolio to editors. "Right away I received some assignments from *Cosmopolitan*, *Elle*, and others, and I couldn't believe my luck," she says. Then she landed a steady job as a magazine designer in Hamburg, Germany, and gained even more experience. This led to more illustration opportunities and to leads in the publishing field. Götz eventually became a full-time freelance artist in Madrid, working for clients such as the *New Yorker*; *Vogue Japan*, *UK and Australia*; *Marie Claire Spain*; and Bloomingdale's.

"My workspace is not ideal at all, it's a rented flat and there's lots of things I would change if I could. But it has good light and lots of shelves, which is great. I find I really don't need the 'perfect' surroundings for working, as long as I'm alone, surrounded by my paper samples, scanner, printer, pencils—and can listen to the radio," says Götz.

Influences

Throughout her career Götz has been inspired by many artists including Ramon Casas, Hiroshige, Erté, and René Gruau. "They all inspire me to seek excellence in what I'm doing: how to find striking graphic solutions, how to treat color, and how to depict the human body in new ways." Color can be problematical. "You change one color, and the whole drawing can fall apart," she says. "Personally I love to use black, especially as a background, because it brings out the other colors, but sadly, I often get restrained by anxious editors who think everything has to be in upbeat spring and summer colors or their product won't sell."

Good Advice

"Be careful what you publish online, because it may haunt you later." She also advises working outside of fashion. "Try to apply your style to as many subjects as possible. That way you'll learn more and keep your work interesting for you and others."

This piece was created as the subject of a short story for the *New Yorker* magazine. The illustration isn't the one that ended up running with the article, but Götz likes this earlier version the best.

A CONNECTION TO HER FANS: NIKI PILKINGTON

Lower East Side, New York, USA

Not everyone will like what you do, and to be honest, it would be a boring world if everyone did!

Niki Pilkington describes her work as playful, detailed portraits of fashion and the girls who wear it. She is known for her pencil portraits and the sculptural elements she adds, something not often seen in fashion illustration. "I like to include three-dimensional elements in my work because the added dimension gives my pieces an extra something that you don't come across very often."

She enjoys the hands-on, crafty part of putting her work together and likes coming up with new ideas. "I'm a sucker for different papers, glues, and tapes. Craft work is always a nice relief from my detailed, slow pace style of drawing. And it's a bonus that I love the final outcome—the shapes and shadows they create on the finished illustrations are always different and always a challenge."

Pilkington starts her pieces by consulting a notebook of ideas, a place where she scribbles down everything from images to words, themes, and colors. "From there I will draw a rough sketch, adding lots of text and I usually make lots of changes once I see the lay-out." There is always strong color in her work and she is fond of neon colors. She almost always renders the faces and detailed sections of the illustration in pencil, preferring to express the rest of the image in color, pattern, and texture. When she is ready to work on the final piece, she always begins with a fresh piece of paper. "I don't like working over roughs because they're always so messy."

CALON
LÂN YN
★ LLAWN ★
DAIONI

"Calon Lân Yn Llawn Daioni/A Pure Heart Full of Joy" (Welsh Song) Graphite, colored pencils and pens. "This is part of a large collection of pieces I created where I researched my Welsh heritage and illustrated old idioms, sayings, and lyrics. This collection continues to grow as I come across more beautiful words and forgotten proverbs each time I return home."

In her young career Niki Pilkington has already worked for some of fashion's top names including Topshop, Sir Paul McCartney, and Ted Baker. For Topshop's London stores, Pilkington created a window display featuring life-size drawings of models dressed in the current collection. For McCartney, she rendered illustrations for a special-edition, remastered album based on his old family photographs. "The photos were scanned at several stages, then animated for a DVD that accompanied the album," she adds.

But it was a genius marketing initiative by fashion house Ted Baker to celebrate the launch of its SS12 campaign that catapulted Pilkington to even more commercial success. The company wanted to collaborate with acclaimed illustrators to create a digital fashion portrait service known as Ted's Drawing Room. Customers tried on pieces from the new Ted Baker collection and posed for a photo in one of the store's photo booths. The images were sent to Pilkington and other illustrators who worked together in a studio drawing their favorite photos. The customers received a digital copy of the illustration and then later a signed, framed original. The entire process was filmed and streamed live on the brand's Facebook page, and people in more than twenty-three countries tuned in to watch the process. "It was very fast paced, and the end result was tons of beautiful portraits in a variety of styles," she says.

Even with the professional success she's received in the commercial world, Pilkington says the most rewarding part of her job is when her work is exhibited and she sees people buying her pieces. "It's always so flattering to hear where they're going to hang them, and what the illustrations represent to them," she says. The connection Pilkington has with fans sets her apart from many illustrators who prefer to stay behind the scenes. She is known for connecting with fans via social media sites, and says online platforms are important to what she does. "I count myself lucky to be able to use the Internet to my advantage. My target audience—mainly young girls and women—is easily reachable this way. I have an online store, and with Twitter, Facebook, and Instagram it's now easier to connect with customers and even clients than it was before," she says. "It's also a nice way to get feedback on what I'm working on. I often post work-in-progress images, and love hearing what people think, as well as being able to offer advice to others who want to know about materials and techniques. I'm always happy to share my thoughts with others."

Influences

"Drawing has always been a big part of what I am and what I've wanted to become," says Pilkington. "The fashion part came along a little later when I realized my love for it and how I could combine the two. I feel I come up with more original ideas when I look away from illustration. I think that's what keeps my work looking special." As a beginner her biggest challenge was coming up with what she wanted to create. "Having a blank page and knowing that I could put absolutely anything on it is the scariest thing of all. Once the idea is figured out, I'm fairly happy to get down to the business of drawing."

Good Advice

It's important not to take criticism to heart. "Try to use it to your advantage and learn from the feedback you get. Don't be afraid of negative comments when you're starting out," Pilkington advises. "Not everyone will like what you do, and to be honest, it would be a boring world if everyone did! Listen to feedback you get, and build from that—and remember, no one likes a show off!"

If This World Only Exists in My Dreams, Don't Wake Me Up "I played with shadows and hidden meanings as part of a collection for an exhibition where I merged nature and fashion, two of my favorite things."

Not All Those Who Wander Are Lost "I've always loved this saying, so I had to put it on paper. The illustration was part of a collection for an exhibition in Wales, where I combined nature, fashion, and typography," notes Pilkington. "I try to add words to my pieces whenever possible. I feel it gives the viewer something to relate to or provides an easier understanding of what I'm trying to say. I also love the combination of delicate drawing and bold typography."

A UNIQUE PERSPECTIVE: GERARDO LARREA

Lima, Peru

I put my characters in a specific scene to interact with each other, creating fun and different situations.

Gerardo Larrea's work not only stands out, its bold lines and colors command attention. He breathes life and energy into his drawings with his use of contrasting colors, the black outlines he prefers, and the shapes he creates. His bold lines give character and strength to his illustrations and work nicely with the graphic style that he captures. "When I started to illustrate my outline was a bit thinner but now I like it bolder."

Larrea usually begins a piece by collecting pictures of the fashion collection he's working on—but he won't read about the designer's inspiration to avoid being biased. He creates small sketches in his notebook, writing down details or thoughts he has about the theme of the work. Then he begins to work up the actual illustration, first with pencil and then delineating the lines with marker, later adding color digitally. He creates the characters first and then works on the background of the piece. "When I'm working on an illustration I work as if I'm taking a fashion editorial photograph and the background is a location or studio integral to the character; for me the background is a tool that helps to reaffirm the concept."

Bold as Love was inspired by the Comme des Garçons FW12 collection, celebrating volume, shape, and color in large proportions.

Gerardo Larrea grew up attending art classes at the Museum of Art in Lima and remembers as a child the fashion magazines his mother read. The drawings, the colors, the silhouettes—and, of course, the fashion—captured his attention.

Although Larrea began creating illustrations for advertisements more than a decade ago, in 2011 he focused on a more defined style for his illustrations. "In my country fashion illustration is new and not a big thing," he says. Still, his work has generated considerable buzz for its graphic style, thick lines, and use of color. "I love color, vivid colors in particular. I love the happiness that color brings to my work," he says.

Who Run the World is inspired by the Chanel FW13 collection and four women who decided to make the world go round; it has a medieval look.

Art Pop Inspired by the Celine SS14 collection. "Characters cross, hide, and reveal, forming a kind of artwork between paint strokes and color," says Larrea.

Influences

Larrea admires the work of Richard Haines, Jordi Labanda, Rubén Toledo, Danny Roberts, and Antonio López. "I think each of them have a particular style, and I love their approach. Each of them has been a real influence in my work." And working as a fashion illustrator, stylist, art director, and fashion editor has helped Larrea develop a unique perspective for his work; interacting so closely with the clothing helps give his illustrations a greater focus on the prints, textures, and details.

Good Advice

"Have passion for your work, believe in yourself, and don't give up."

The Fight Club depicts two sophisticated and powerful women, showing off their strength in a boxing ring.

Here Comes the Sun inspired by the Peter Som SS14 Collection, shows three women on a summer day at the beach.

MAKING A NAME:
YAEKO ABE

New Jersey, USA

Being loose and spontaneous is my favorite way of drawing.

Yaeko Abe's intricate line drawings reflect a refined simplicity not often seen in fashion illustration. When drawing for himself he doesn't create any preliminary sketches but on client-commissioned pieces he will create several rounds of sketches. "After I get an approval on a sketch, I move on to the final drawing, usually using a black ink pen or a calligraphy pen." Abe often uses different types of ink pens, and later adds colors with markers before adjusting the final piece in Photoshop. "Being loose and spontaneous is my favorite way of drawing," he says.

Yaeko Abe is one of fashion illustration's newest talents. The New Jersey artist began to illustrate professionally in 2012, and became interested in pursuing it as a career while attending the Fashion Institute of Technology. He has created illustrations for *Elle Girl Japan* and *Elle Russia* magazines and a mural for British fashion company New Look.

Hair Power "This was a result of looking at hairstyle magazines and wanting to experiment with typography without thinking too much about the mechanical aspect of it," Abe says.

Influences

The works of British illustrator Aubrey Beardsley, author and artist Shel Silverstein, and illustrator Annika Wester, have all had an impact on Abe, but he says figuring out his own style was, and still is, his biggest struggle because he likes to explore different materials and a variety of subject matter.

Good Advice

"Keep on illustrating and utilize all your time. Also, be polite to even the meanest of clients."

Breeze "I really wanted to use the blue pen in my collections of colorful pens, and this was something that fit the image of the color at the time," says Yaeko Abe.

Fashion Collage
"I created this during one Fashion Week after seeing great outfits all around the streets."

SOPHISTICATED GLAMOUR: LUIS TINOCO

Barcelona, Spain

Enjoy your work and make others enjoy it too.

Luis Tinoco always starts a sketch in pencil to create an initial impression. Then he applies color, and later retouches the piece digitally. He calls his illustration style realism and sophisticated glamour, using watercolors and paint to create a fresh and contemporary fashion style.

Tinoco says the colors he uses in his work change depending on what he is creating and what the fashion color trends are each season. Although in his watercolor work, lines are often absent, with other mediums he will incorporate noticeable lines to create depth and to accentuate forms or highlight a specific area of the illustration.

Luis Tinoco has been drawing since he was a child but his interest in fashion came later when he began working in advertising agencies as an art director, which has led to his work on client accounts such as Carolina Herrera, Rimmel, and United Colors of Benetton, among others. His work encompasses everything from illustrations for a cartoon series to childrens' books to illustrations for the biggest names in beauty and fashion including *Glamour Spain* and *Glamour Germany* magazines.

Juicy Couture Here, Tinoco was inspired by 1950s summer fashion.

Christian Louboutin
This is Tinoco's take on the fashion-forward shoes.

Influences

Like other contemporary illustrators, Tinoco cites the legendary master of fashion illustration René Gruau as an influence, as well as top fashion designers such as John Galliano, Alexander McQueen, Jean Paul Gaultier, and Marc Jacobs. But during his early years as an illustrator he worked to find his own style—one that would offer a different and creative point of view and set him apart from other fashion illustrators.

Good Advice

For Tinoco, one of the biggest challenges as a fashion illustrator is keeping abreast of all the fashion trends in an industry that changes seasonally and has new colors, fabrics, models, styles, and designers all the time. "Enjoy your work and make others enjoy it too."

Kate Moss, God Save the Queen This watercolor and digital illustration was inspired by British pop culture.

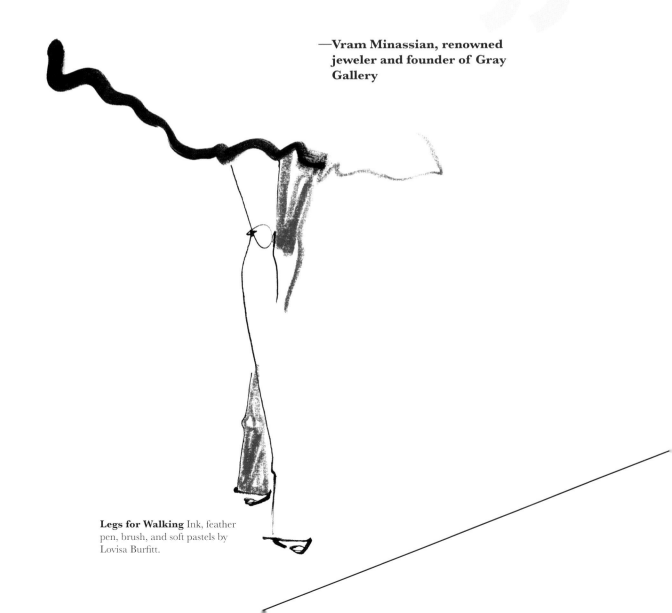

Fashion illustrations are the prelude to our understanding of the product. They are able to stimulate the imagination— to leave space for diverse interpretations of the style.

—Vram Minassian, renowned
    jeweler and founder of Gray
    Gallery

Legs for Walking Ink, feather
pen, brush, and soft pastels by
Lovisa Burfitt.

PART 2
THE ICONS

THE BEAUTY OF IMPERFECTION: DANNY ROBERTS

Laguna Niguel, California, USA

> **For the most part, I think and visualize in black and white.**

Danny Roberts creates his illustrations using a technique called blind contour, which involves looking at the paper as little as possible and instead keeping his gaze on the inspiration piece. He uses pen, ink, watercolors, and mixed media for his illustrations. Roberts is known for the special quality of his line work. His lines are confident; some play with size—he makes them thicker or thinner for added dimension—and some play with edges—which are seemingly invisible or unfinished, allowing the viewer's imagination to fill in the rest. Color is often an afterthought for Roberts. "For the most part, I think and visualize in black and white," he says. "My use of [color] is very different depending on the piece. I usually use it as a tool to highlight or contrast parts of the piece."

Danny Roberts, who along with his brother David is the creative team behind Igor + Andre, began illustrating while in college. In a short time, the native Californian's work has been featured in some of the most elite fashion magazines in the world, including *Teen Vogue*, *Vogue Italia*, *Vogue Paris*, *Vogue Japan*, *Elle*, and *Women's Wear Daily*. While still in his twenties, he forged deals with some of the biggest names in fashion, illustrating a line of Gwen Stefani's Harajuku Lover's handbags and forming a partnership with Forever 21 that showcased his fashion illustrations of bloggers on T-shirts. He also worked with IMG Models to illustrate the fresh faces debuting in an upcoming runway season.

Girls in Glasses An illustration of girls wearing Chanel glasses that has been adapted for T-shirts.

Roberts' pencil, pen, colored pencil, ink, watercolor, and oil paint drawing with clothes from Marchesa's Fall 2012 collection.

One of the highlights of his illustration career featured his work on a much larger scale—literally. When famed jewelry house Tiffany & Co. began building its SoHo, New York store, it commissioned Roberts to illustrate the façade of the construction site with a beautiful scene of women and men dressed in elegant ball gowns and stylish suits. The project, which took approximately 133 hours to complete and measured 15 x 35 feet (4.6 x 10.7 m), is the largest project Roberts has worked on.

A Moment in Love A commissioned mural for Tiffany & Co.

Roberts's studio space.

Influences

Danny Roberts calls fashion the door into a dream world. He has an inspiration library of more than 150,000 images on his computer, admires fashion photographers Man Ray and Steven Meisel, and counts models Gemma Ward and Lily Cole as two of his illustration muses. Although fashion, especially the modeling world, often demands perfection and software programs have made it possible to blur photographs to hide human flaws, Roberts says illustration is making a comeback because people are drawn to imperfections. He says imperfections mimic our own lives. When an image is perfect, it's harder for people to connect with it.

Roberts had always been interested in fashion—he even started a T-shirt company when he was in junior high school—but it wasn't until he was studying fashion design at San Francisco's Academy of Art University that he found and nurtured his talent for illustration. He fell in love with drawing in his first figure drawing class. Although he always doodled as a kid, he says, "It was in that class that I really learned to draw." And once he committed to drawing every day, his work improved.

At first, Roberts admits it was strange to get started, mostly "because I wasn't quite sure how." A big break came when he was commissioned to create an Alexander McQueen portrait for a *Sunday Times* magazine cover story that chronicled the famous designer's final days. Roberts says McQueen has had the most influence on his work.

Good Advice

Roberts advises artists to "practice every day, and don't judge a piece until it is finished."

The Velvet Dress Girl Design was created for Roberts's "What's Contemporary" collection and was featured in *L'Officiel* magazine.

EXPRESSING PERSONAL STYLE AND DESIGN: JAD BAGHDADI

Los Angeles and San Francisco, California, USA

Find your voice and try to perfect it.

Sometimes Jad Baghdadi will drape fabric on a mannequin for ideas and silhouette inspiration for an illustration, other times he will reference old sketches and art. He works on loose sheets of paper, which tend to pile up in his studio. He has a distinct illustration style; his technique includes using exaggerated movements in the subject and silhouetting it—in fact, not being afraid to exaggerate the subject's form is some of the best advice Baghdadi says he's ever received. The use of color in his work depends on the subject, but he tends to incorporate vibrant colors within loose bold lines. "Find your voice and try to perfect it," he advises.

Jad Baghdadi has been illustrating since he was a teenager. "I'm a [fashion] designer, so illustration was always the perfect way to express my personal style and designs," he says.

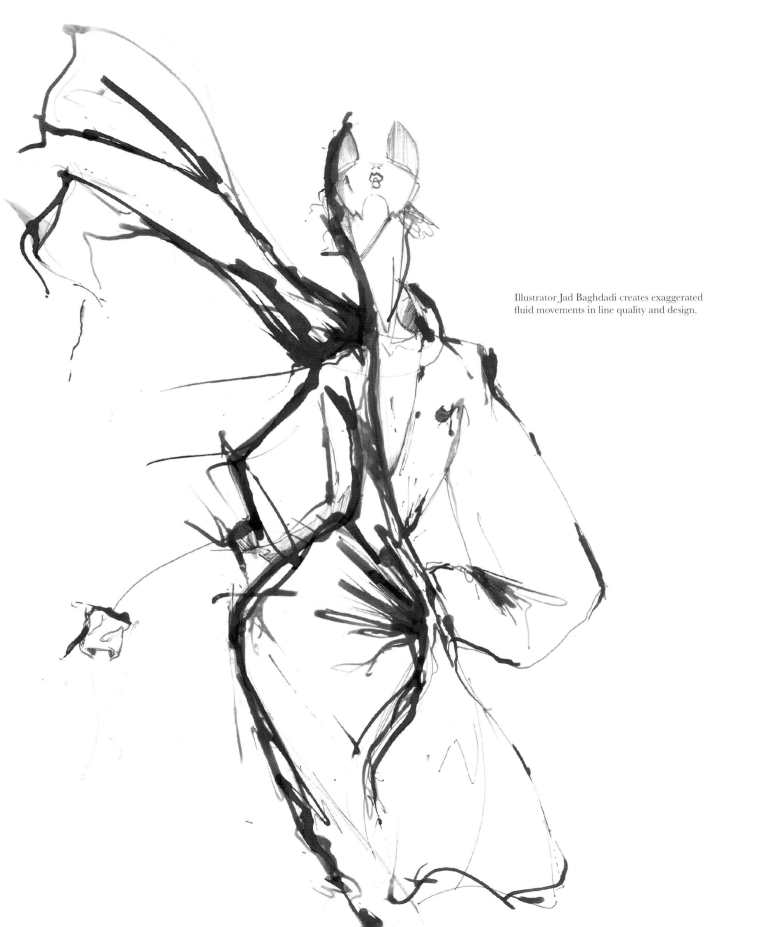

Illustrator Jad Baghdadi creates exaggerated fluid movements in line quality and design.

In the few years since graduating from Academy of Art University in San Francisco, Baghdadi has risen to some of the top spots in fashion, working in design and illustration at Monique Lhuillier, Herve Leger, and Zac Posen. "Starting out, I submitted my portfolio to a number of design houses looking for internships and work," he says. His first big break was landing an internship at Zac Posen. "That was a great, eye-opening experience for me as a designer and a fashion illustrator."

Illustrator Jad Baghdadi creates exaggerated silhouettes with abstract layered lines.

Influences

Baghdadi's inspiration comes from fashion icons such as David Downton, Richard Gray, Tom Ford, Giambattista Valli, and Elie Saab.

Illustrator Jad Baghdadi creates a bold line movement accented with a delicate fading quality.

AN EMPHASIS ON THE BEAUTY OF FASHION: MICHAEL HOEWELER

Brooklyn, New York, USA

Invest in the relationships you develop with art directors, designers, and other like-minded professionals who seek you out for work.

Michael Hoeweler starts a new work by drawing small sketches in his sketchbook and planning out the image in his mind. "After I have a solid composition, I seek out reference images and take photographs to help root the illustration in reality." Once the general idea of the illustration is planned out, Hoeweler will size up the sketch on a larger piece of paper, and draft an underdrawing with graphite pencil. Then he finalizes the illustration working in graphite only, or finishes the drawing with sumi ink and pen.

"I like color, and I use it when I'm asked to, but most of the work I do in my spare time is exclusively black and white. I tend to work with color semi-realistically, or as an accent wash to lay over a black and white illustration," he notes. Once an illustration is finished, Hoeweler scans the final and does any needed edits in Photoshop. He calls his technique "traditional, with a digital finish."

Michael Hoeweler is known for striking black and white illustrations that showcase the clothing's smallest details. When beginning a piece, Hoeweler says, "I write out words, ideas, and content that I would like to focus on. I also write the narrative of the illustration and what I want to communicate."

Michael Hoeweler sketchbook.

Hoeweler lays out the figure and composes the main subject matter in the illustration. He draws in the clothing over the figure, tightens the drawing, and begins laying down flat areas of watercolor.

He keeps applying washes of watercolor until he feels that the atmosphere and the tone is right. In the process, the graphite drawing becomes faint.

He goes back in with graphite and charcoal to bring the original drawing to the surface, adding in small details as he works.

As the final drawing comes together, Hoeweler goes back in with gouache to bring out the light source and highlight details, such as the bead work in the gown. After it is complete he edits the illustration digitally.

He has worked with publications including *Time, GQ, Travel + Leisure,* and the *Washington Post,* and has been commissioned by Brooks Brothers to draw menswear illustrations for its website. "Brooks Brothers was looking for a softer, more nuanced approach than my editorial work, and the work for them proved to be an exciting step toward merging two of my techniques: sumi ink and graphite."

Influences

While studying art at Maryland Institute College of Art in Baltimore, Hoeweler created illustrations for *Out* magazine. The art director helped him hone in on techniques and approaches that were both distinctive and commercially viable. "I really learned that fashion illustration can be just as thoughtful, conceptual, and creative as any other kind of illustration. The art director's advice opened up a world of possibility to me, and allowed me to make fashion illustration about more than just beautiful clothing. While I was at the magazine, I also met some great editors who would become future clients."

When Hoeweler was first developing his style, he looked at the work of late nineteenth-century European painters. "Edgar Degas, Édouard Manet, Édouard Vuillard, and Henri de Toulouse-Lautrec were constantly in my mind," he says. Hoeweler also closely follows the work of Christophe Lemaire for Hermés, Alber Elbaz for Lanvin, Sarah Burton for Alexander McQueen, sisters Kate and Laura Mulleavy for Rodarte, Raf Simons for Christian Dior, and Riccardo Tisci for Givenchy. "Their processes involve heavy research, intensive craftsmanship, and thoughtful execution. Their concepts are highly developed, and they focus on experimentation within and outside of the traditions of clothing. I love that."

Although Hoeweler is now courted for his illustration style, during his first couple of years he says the thing that challenged him the most was composition. "I tend to get ahead of myself and skip the planning that should come before an illustration. My understanding of balance and image development was largely intuitive then, and I should have been more conscious of the decisions I was making. I've grown since then, but it's a constant source of development for me."

Look 35, a runway study of a look from Giambattista Valli, by Michael Hoeweler.

Working with the inspirations and concepts behind Rodarte's Fall 2010 collection, Michael Hoeweler's illustration memorializes the women who worked at the *maquiladoras*, the factories, in Juárez, Mexico.

Good Advice

"Illustration is a career where diligence and perseverance pay off. Never underestimate your ability to draw. Learn as much as you can about traditional, figurative drawing and take life-drawing courses. Even if your interests, approaches, or style move further away from reality, knowing how to draw well gives you the groundwork you need to focus on your ideas. Finally, invest in the relationships you develop with art directors, designers, and other like-minded professionals who seek you out for work. They deserve utmost respect, appreciation, consideration, and kindness."

Sweeter Than Heaven, Hotter Than Hell shows Florence Welch, from the band Florence + the Machine, dressed in a gown from Gucci's fall 2011 collection, which was inspired by the singer.

A FEMININE, COLORFUL STYLE: SAMANTHA HAHN

Brooklyn, New York, USA

Everything you do should look like it was done with the same hand even if you use a variety of media and styles.

Samantha Hahn's style is a decidedly feminine mix of delicate quill lines with an economy of lush and vibrant watercolor. She begins her work by finding references or taking a photograph to capture the physicality or expression she wants to use. She will search for fabric textures or patterns to reference before she begins painting. "With watercolor, you only have one chance to get it right, so if the illustration isn't working, I'll just paint it over and over until it clicks," she says. Her aim is to make it look effortless with an efficient use of lines and shapes. Then she will scan the piece into Photoshop and play with it digitally, sizing it and enhancing or modifying the colors, before sending it to her agency or the client.

"At first the illustration world seems vast and you have to find your point of entry and carve out your niche in the market," recalls Samantha Hahn. Through trial and error and her willingness to accept rejection and learn from it, to grow and try again, she found her voice. Once you are situated firmly in the industry, she says, work will beget work. "That's where I am now," she says. "Instead of spending a huge portion of my time trying to get work, I spend it doing projects that more clients will see. When your work is published it's like a public vetting. Clients find you and see what you can do and believe that you will perform well for them as well."

Her work includes a published book, *Well-Read Women: Portraits of Fiction's Most Beloved Heroines*, a collection of 50 of her evocative illustrations, and commissions from clients such as Refinery 29, *New York* magazine, *The Cut*, and *Vogue Nippon*.

The Row

Marchesa by
Samantha Hahn

Influences

Hahn admires Andy Warhol's early illustration work for the renowned shoe company, I. Miller and *Harper's Bazaar.* "I also love the artists who worked in the heyday of illustration: Maxfield Parrish and Coles Phillips," she says. Clients often hire her for the watercolor and ink style she uses in fashion and beauty but she has illustrated for a range of clients with different objectives. "I recently completed a series of black ink illustrations for the *Paris Review.* I like to try different things, but I'm known for my feminine, colorful watercolor illustrations." Hahn says she is obsessed with color and isn't afraid to explore or experiment. She loves playing with palettes from warm monochromes to pops of cool jewel tones.

Good Advice

"Put the work you love doing out there and it will speak for itself. Hone your skills. Get your craft to where your taste is. If you are going to make it in the market you have to have the taste to know what's good and why the professional artists are getting work," Hahn says. "When you are doing good work, target it to companies and publications you want to work with and pound the proverbial pavement with your portfolio until you start getting work. Work begets work. Give yourself dream projects and imagine who your client is. Make your site and your portfolio look as professional as possible. Everything you do should look like it was done with the same hand even if you use a variety of media and styles. Don't be afraid to submit and submit. Eventually you will knock on the right door and it will open for you. The cream rises to the top," she says.

VIVID AND ELEGANT: STINA PERSSON

Stockholm, Sweden

> **Develop a personal style and seek inspiration not from other illustrators but fine artists.**

Stina Persson may be one of the most well-respected and widely known female illustrators. She works in many mediums and her techniques include drawing, painting, collage, and—when necessary—the computer. "I draw a gazillion sketches and then choose the best one to work on," she notes. "I love working with color and it comes to me easily, which is why I do lots of watercolor. Of course, I also love the rawness and edginess of ink, as well as the structural feel of collage."

Stina Persson studied fine art and fashion in Italy. While studying fashion design and "feeling like a misfit," her drawing teacher suggested illustration. Luckily, for the art and fashion world she followed his advice, moved to New York, and studied illustration. It took time for Persson to be successful, but a teacher at the renowned Pratt Institute in Brooklyn prepared her, explaining that it takes three years until work comes in steadily—and when it happened more quickly, she was thrilled.

Blonde "This was originally made for the online gallery Wonderwall, but they ended up choosing a different piece," Persson says. "I had been listening to a lot of '80s music and was inspired by the drama and the absence of irony. This piece reflects how I think: bold, big, wide, and a bit over the top. I used thick brushes and the wrong end of the brush for the thin lines. The color in the top is pieces of red acetate."

Influences

Although her own style is unique and has been called a fusion of traditional and edgy, introducing a modern look to illustration, Persson counts her friends and colleagues Sara Singh, Tina Berning, and Cecilia Carlstedt, and eminent masters such as Antonio Lopez, René Gruau, and Paul Rand as influences.

She notes that the field of illustration is a lot bigger than people might think. "Most of my clients don't come from the fashion world, but just want illustrations with flair and a contemporary look," she says. Over the years Persson has worked with top magazines *Vogue Nippon*, *Harper's Bazaar*, *Elle UK*, and *Marie Claire*, and corporate retailers American Eagle Outfitters, Bloomingdale's, and Macy's.

Good Advice

"Take any job you can get. But never work for nothing. A client will never pay for something they earlier got for free, no matter what they promise," she says. "Develop a personal style and seek inspiration not from other illustrators but fine artists."

Bearskin Hat A piece for Reebok Brazil. "They wanted a set of illustrations in a René Gruau style. It was a really fun and creative process."

Ava One of twenty-five pieces Persson created for her New York show Perfectly Flawed. "This is as much a portrait of a boldly printed tunic as it is of a woman. All pieces in the show were originals."

EVOLVING STYLE: LULU*

Berlin, Germany

**"It is all about high quality
work, and good use of color.**

LULU* is known for her hand-drawn illustrations that she describes as retro minimalist combined with a '60s vibe and finely tuned digital work. Her illustration process begins with an analog sketch, and when she feels the image is right, she will scan it and work in Photoshop to develop it further. She says her work has evolved over the years and she likes the idea of changing and trying new things.

LULU* does it all. She creates illustrations for advertising, animation, and editorial design, but considers fashion the most beautiful and poetic of all the fields. Her first impressions of form and color were formed in her mother's flower shop in Solingen, Germany, but it was while studying at the College of Fine Arts at the University of Künste in Berlin—where Vivienne Westwood was a professor—that she immersed herself in fashion drawing.

After working for Tyler Brûlé, founder of the famed fashion magazine *Wallpaper*, at his branding and advertising agency Winkreative, LULU* became known as one of Germany's illustration talents, creating pieces for clients such as Bloomingdale's, Swarovski, *Vogue Pelle*, and *Vogue Nippon*.

Illustration by LULU*.

Inspired by the look of Balmain Paris, LULU* says in this piece, "Working with positive and negative space was my aim."

Influences

"The Internet is a huge ocean where you sometimes can get stuck," she says, "but it's also a great place to share art projects, images, and music to help inspire and be inspired." She loves to visit art exhibitions and counts artists such as Egon Schiele and Andy Warhol as inspirations.

Good Advice

"It is all about high quality work, and good use of color." LULU* says she always has a feeling about which colors are appropriate in a piece.

LULU* says, "The Flair Mondatori outfits were based on different looks you can wear for the most hip clubs in Vienna. The women were supposed to be elegant and self-confident. The patterns were very beautiful to draw."

A STORIED CAREER:
JULIE JOHNSON

Jeddah, Saudi Arabia

> **Stop drawing well before you think the illustration is done. It remains fresher that way, and an overworked drawing makes the viewers less able to fill in the details with their imagination.**

Julie Johnson always starts a piece by painting or drawing it by hand first and then scanning the drawing so she can build layers digitally. "Sometimes I like a neutral palette of earthy colors, sometimes I like blacks, fuchsias and whites. In looking at art and nature, color is what excites me most."

She prefers to draw from a live model, but says she can easily work from her own photographs or from memory. "I use the computer very little, except for layering color and line, turning a piece into digital form for a client, or archiving my work."

Julie Johnson has been an illustrator for more than three decades. Looking back at the start of her career she says, "There was no digital technology and no Internet. Bloomingdale's in New York would send over clothes by bike messenger, and I'd hire a model to pose in them, do drawings, and send the drawings back with the clothes by bike messenger. Within a day or two the art would appear in Bloomingdale's ads in the *New York Times.* Illustrators would walk their portfolio around to different agencies and clients to find more work."

Redhead One of a series of illustrations for retailer Filene's Basement displayed at the Union Square subway station, New York.

Johnson

Johnson has studied at the San Francisco Art Institute, the Academy of Art University in San Francisco, and Parsons: The New School for Design in New York. She has won four awards from the Society of Illustrators in New York for "Best of Fashion Illustration," as well as an award from the *Communication Arts Illustration Annual*. "It's nice to be formally recognized by the field, however, achievement is also measured in the ability to make a living at what you love to do, and I have had many long-term contracts with clients," she says. "I loved seeing my work for Filene's Basement over a five-year period at the Union Square subway station in New York, as well as on city kiosks and displayed on the sides of buildings. I feel that each year has brought different achievements and I continually look for more."

Julie Johnson sketchbooks

Gianfranco Ferré Julie Johnson's illustration of a Ferré sheer and paneled blouse.

John
Beaumonde

Julie Johnson's studio space.

Influences

"I have always been fascinated by people, clothing, culture, shape, silhouette, and color—and I've always loved to draw and paint. All these disparate loves seemed to converge in fashion illustration," Johnson says. She draws inspiration from many areas including her love of travel, especially to Africa and Asia, and her appreciation of the clothing of other cultures, especially Tibetan, Native American, and Japanese.

Good Advice

In her extensive career, the best advice Johnson has received about illustrating fashion is, "Stop drawing well before you think the illustration is done. It remains fresher that way, and an overworked drawing makes the viewers less able to fill in the details with their imagination." Her advice for emerging talents is to remember that talent will only take you so far. "You need to have a continued drive and passion for what you are doing. Don't imitate illustrators of the past, make your own statement, and use your own being and viewpoint to inform your art. Love doing it."

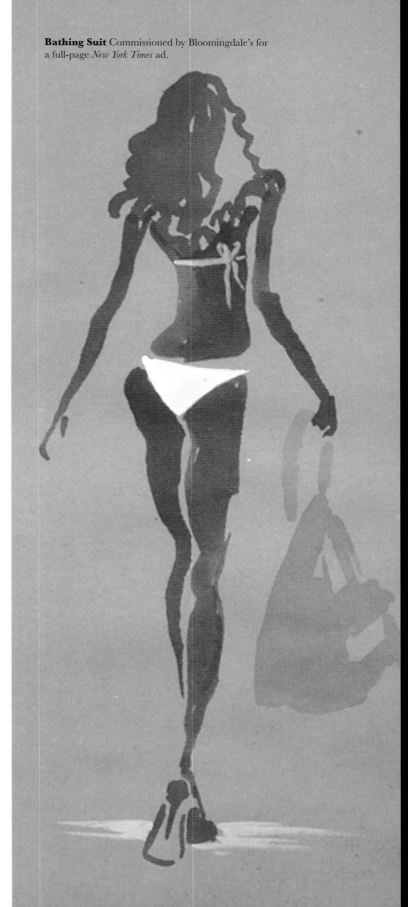

Bathing Suit Commissioned by Bloomingdale's for a full-page *New York Times* ad.

STAYING TRUE:
NUNO DA COSTA

Lisbon, Portugal

**I couldn't imagine a life
without drawing in it.**

Nuno Da Costa starts his work researching images in magazines and books. He then creates a loose sketch, which can be reworked a couple of times before he's satisfied with it. He scans the final pencil drawing and prints it on bristol board so he can paint it with gouache and watercolors. When he feels it's where he wants it to be, he scans the painted illustration and prints it. Sometimes he will also paint over the print. "You can get really attached to how your work looks and you can be scared to mess it up, and this really removes that fear."

Vogue always meant something to Nuno Da Costa. To him it has always been synonymous with style, elegance, and quality, and he dreamed that he would one day be good enough to be published in its pages. "I knew when I started illustrating that I wasn't ready or good enough but I told myself that if I worked hard and stayed true to who I am as an illustrator that I could make it happen." It took ten years but he got his work published in *British Vogue*.

He is known for the "Nuno woman" and he says she is growing and maturing as he does. "She's strong and vulnerable, modern and classic, with an edge to her. She's complex and contradictory, as we all are. I'm learning to let go, to let her and my work go—to be not so perfect," Da Costa explains.

Illustration by Nuno Da Costa

Illustration by Nuno Da Costa

LOUIS
VUTTON

Influences

At a young age Da Costa was attracted to the
drawings on packaging and in comic books
and always loved fashion. "Fashion wasn't ev-
erywhere as it is today," he says. "My parents
didn't buy fashion magazines. I used to watch
this one show on television every weekend
called *The Clothes Show* with my mum when I
was little. I would lie on the floor drawing the
models as they walked past. One of my ear-
liest memories is watching the *Valentino* show
and drawing the model in a red dress."

Good Advice

For Da Costa, starting out in the field was exciting, nerve-wracking, and exhilarating. "Illustration is really a personal thing and it communicates details about your inner self that you can't explain or put into words, and to have that out there for people to critique can be daunting." He says beginning illustrators should not judge themselves too harshly or compare themselves to others—something he says he is still trying to learn. "Illustration isn't about who draws the best, it's about finding your own voice, your own language. It sounds cheesy but it is so true; it's not our job to be anyone else, we just have to be the best 'self' that we can."

Fashion illustration, like life, is a journey, says Da Costa, and an ongoing process of learning and exploring your skill, your taste, and yourself. He recommends setting goals for yourself no matter how unattainable they may seem. "Dare to dream big and be prepared to work hard to achieve that dream. Know that rejection is temporary and part of the process, and that one day you will look back and understand why things happened the way they did. Use rejection as fuel to get you from A to B."

Illustration by Nuno Da Costa

BREAK THE RULES: LOVISA BURFITT

Aix-en-Provence, France

I'll walk around the task until I bite into it. Once I get started I think, 'OK, maybe I can do this.'

Lovisa Burfitt often creates her illustrations using a metal feather that she dips in Chinese ink. She also likes to mix what she calls high and low, using inexpensive pencils with dry pastels and colored pens on beautiful, expensive paper. She often uses the classic color pairing of black and red. "I'm always fascinated with the palette of colors that other artists use and how they thought of that. I love a sharp vermillion red, almost an orange, and I often find myself coming back to that." When she has completed a sketch that she's really happy with she'll put it in her archive. "I used to throw them away when I was finished, but if I draw a pose that I like, I keep it because I may draw from it again. But sometimes the sketches are really ugly, then you just have to throw them away."

Lovisa Burfitt has been illustrating professionally for almost two decades, but her interest in fashion started as a young child. "I would sew my own clothes out of mum's old curtain and I would make a skirt from dad's old leather jacket," she says. "When I was about eleven, a friend asked if I was going to be a fashion designer when I grew up," says the Swedish illustrator, who now lives in the south of France. "I asked him what that was and he said it was someone who made clothes for a living—so I said yes. I made the decision then to become a designer and I kind of just stuck with it."

Warm Leatherette Ink, aquarelle, and Posca pen.

Influences

With the encouragement of her father, Burfitt went to fashion school where she studied to be a designer but took many classes in fashion illustration. "I had a teacher who would give us a brief when we had an assignment. She would say, 'Of course you can misunderstand, please misunderstand, do misunderstand.' She meant that it was important to interpret the assignment in our own way, to use our imagination. For me it worked to break the rules." Burfitt remembers school as a place where she was pushed to try new techniques and experiment with style. "You would bring your favorite paper and pens and brushes to class, and then the teacher would tell you to swap with the person next to you. You were confronted with what to do with this brush you weren't familiar with. It was a really good way of learning."

After college, Burfitt moved to Paris, started her own clothing line, and began to draw more—combining her interest in fashion with illustration. With the help of an agent, she began receiving illustration commissions from some of the top names in the fashion and beauty industry. Burfitt is known largely for her work with *Vogue*, *Elle*, *Glamour*, and *Grazia* magazines, beauty brands Guerlain and Sephora, and another Swedish import—retail giant H&M. "It was really fun and free working with H&M," she says. Burfitt created an archive of more than 120 drawings that the brand uses on the walls of its stores around the world, including Singapore, Tokyo, Athens, New York, and London. "I like their attitude and it was important to them to signal to the client that fashion is fun. They like a touch of humor, which suits me a lot."

Mlle Fatale Rouge Pouf Ink, feather pen, brush, and colored pencil.

Nice 2013 Ink, feather pen, brush, and colored pencil.

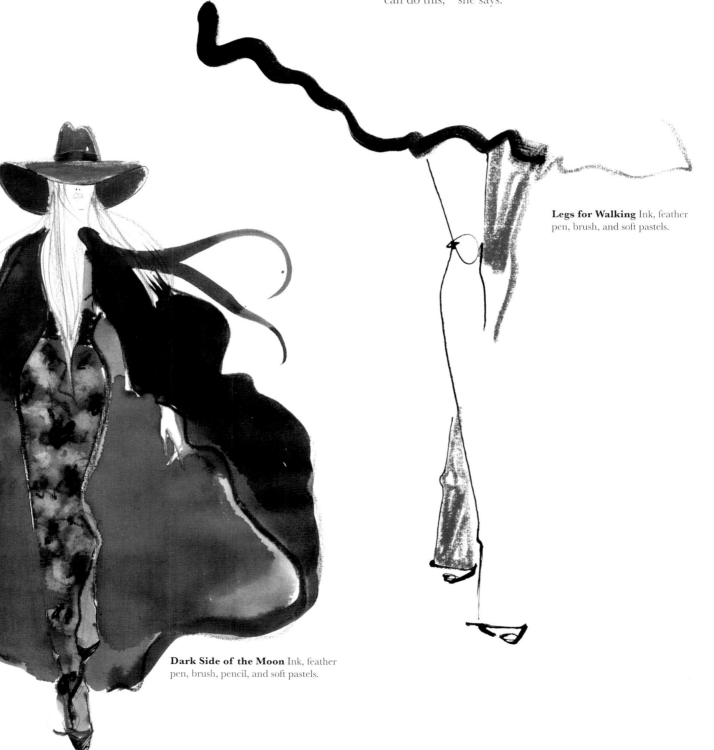

Good Advice

"I need to be totally in my artistic bubble, to turn off everything else, when I draw, so I usually play loud music. I find it difficult to work when people talk to me when I draw. I'll walk around the task until I bite into it. Once I get started I think, 'OK, maybe I can do this,'" she says.

Legs for Walking Ink, feather pen, brush, and soft pastels.

Dark Side of the Moon Ink, feather pen, brush, pencil, and soft pastels.

La Isla Bonita 2013 Ink, feather pen, brush, colored pencil, and soft pastels.

COLLABORATION:
WILL BROOME

London, England

Be nice and work hard.

The light box is the most high-tech piece of equipment Will Broome uses. His hand-drawn works are recognizable for their quirky characters that make you want to smile.

Broome tries not to plan too much, and just waits to see where the drawing will take him; he prefers not to do research and not to cloud his mind with an abundance of noise. "I'm not saying I work in a total vacuum. There are things and artists that interest me and inspire me but I prefer to just sit down and draw," he says. For example, when working with a client he collaborates with them through the drawing process, showing them what he's doing, discussing the many iterations and ideas the piece goes through, and the finished piece evolves from that process. "I think that's what a collaboration is about. It's the way I like to work," he says.

He will go through a phase where he works in black and white only, then will start working with loads of color. "I'm not sure why. I think it might have to do with the weather. I hate the winter; I don't like the early dark nights."

Exhibited work by illustrator Will Broome.

Exhibited work by illustrator Will Broome.

Will Broome's success has been due in part to undeniable talent and in part to a bit of serendipity. The first person he worked with was Marc Jacobs, creating drawings used on T-shirts and stickers. Broome had just broken up with his girlfriend at the time and was devastated. He spent time lying on his couch watching movies on mute while listening to songs about heartbroken lovers. A college friend who was designing for Marc Jacobs asked Broome to do some drawings for the brand—her way, he believes, of trying to lift him out of his despair. He created a sketchbook in what he says was a very absentminded way. "I didn't think 'this is my big break' or anything like that. I wasn't thinking straight at the time, never mind being able to plot world domination! Besides, I think that if I'd created the book thinking 'this could lead to something' then the drawings wouldn't be as good." The Marc Jacobs brand loved the drawings and the next thing Broome knew his work was coming to life on the runway at New York Fashion Week.

Artist Will Broome's studio space.

PASSION:
CAROLINE ANDRIEU

Paris, France

Be involved in each project as if it is the most important one ever.

Caroline Andrieu usually uses colored inks or just simple pencils in her work. "I started to work with lots of ink in my first fashion illustrations. I like that you can't erase it, that you have to deal with your mistakes, with the stains. The ink actually gives a lot of strength to the pictures. Later, when I was given a big box of colored pencils, which I hated so much when I was a kid, I started drawing with them and enjoyed it right away. The technique is very different from ink or watercolor—it is more subtle, less free, in a way. I now try to draw with both techniques on my illustrations." Andrieu doesn't sketch a lot, unless the client needs to see something first. Instead she likes to finish an illustration the same day she starts it. "I'm not very patient. I have to be in the same mood all the way through the process, otherwise I may not finish it. I draw rather quickly so that's not a problem for now. But I would like to work on bigger surfaces so I have to learn patience, I think."

Caroline Andrieu started working as an illustrator little by little. She began her career as a graphic designer and was drawing just for herself. After showing illustrations to friends, and starting to share what she was creating on a blog, news of her work spread on social networks and she landed her first clients. As the art director of Condé Nast Digital France, for the *Vogue* and *GQ* websites, she was surrounded by fashion so it was natural to include more fashion in her illustrations.

Influences

Andrieu is a fan of artists Hans Bellmer and David Hockney as well as, more recently, of the work of Charles Burns, Elizabeth Peyton, and Michael Gillette. She is also inspired by contemporary photography.

Good Advice

"Be passionate. Fashion illustration is evolving every day, more and more, and I am glad to be part of it."

Daiane Conterato for Dries Van Noten Spring 2014, ink and pencil, by Caroline Andrieu (far left).
Kel Markey for Proenza Schouler Spring 2013, color pencils, by Caroline Andrieu (left).
Mariacarla Boscono for Hermes Fall 2014, color pencils, by Caroline Andrieu (top, left).
Lindsey Wixson for Prada Spring 2014, watercolor by Caroline Andrieu (above).
Nastya Sten for Alexandar McQueen Spring 2014, color pencils by Caroline Andrieu (right).

DESTINED FOR ILLUSTRATION: AUTUMN WHITEHURST

Brooklyn, New York, USA

Honestly, I think sometimes that I create the illustrations only to provide me with an opportunity to work with color, it's the thing that I enjoy most about my work.

Whitehurst's labor-intensive process starts with pencil sketches to generate ideas and with thorough research on the Internet, but the bulk of her work is created with a stash of modern digital tools. She will create a tight sketch in Illustrator and then play with the pose, proportions, and composition. "I ask my clients to make any major revisions at this point because once I bring the vector file into Photoshop to render different elements, it's a tremendous amount of work to make changes."

Her client list is as diverse as the restaurant Sapporo and the Principality of Monaco, but the pieces that are dearest to her are the ones she has done for the *Telegraph Magazine*. She says: "The illustrations have to be turned out fairly quickly because the magazine is a weekly, so I really had to streamline my efforts, and have learned a lot from working in these circumstances."

Autumn Whitehurst was destined to be a fashion illustrator—although the Brooklyn–based artist admits she wasn't particularly focused on becoming one at first. After putting together a small selection of images and posting them on an online portfolio site, the work began to find her.

Have fun with color. "I've yet to push it far enough, though. The way that the colors in a palette, or the lack of them, are used helps determine how we engage with the image. At the moment I'm really enjoying colors that are acidic, tart, or dry."

Lux is a self-promotion piece about luxury.

"My boyfriend and I share the studio," says Autumn Whitehurst of her illustration workspace. "The studio looks really peaceful, but the building is flanked by a construction company and a distribution warehouse, so there are a lot of trucks beeping and engines idling."

Balmain is an illustration created for an article about an iconic Balmain dress.

TENACITY:
ERIN PETSON

London, England

> **Really find your style. It defines you and makes you stand out from the crowd.**

When possible, Petson starts her illustrations using a model. If she's not working with a model, she references a huge library of photographs from her personal photo-shoot archive. She creates a sketch, making light and heavy marks with a pencil, adding abstract marks and color to create the shapes and colors she sees in the garment and the figure. "Color can be very intimidating because you don't want to ruin your pencil drawing. But once you add color, it gives the illustration enough structure that you don't always have to draw in line." After her sketch is complete, she scans the work to digitally manipulate the scale or composition in Photoshop.

Erin Petson has been illustrating professionally for more than a decade. In the beginning she says it was incredibly hard but she was hungry for success, and she nurtured a drive that would continue throughout her entire career. "I loved sending out postcards to fashion houses and getting responses, even if they were not the desired response," she says. To try to get work, Petson approached local businesses with her drawings, and the result was her first gigs with boutiques and hair salons. Her big break came when she moved to London and landed a job with luxury department store Selfridges designing window displays. In the years since, she has been invited by Dior to contribute to an exhibition about René Gruau at Somerset House in London, and the Victoria and Albert Museum has archived sixty of her original drawings.

Fashion Ink, pastel, pencil, graphite, acrylic by Erin Petson.

Love Elise Ink, pastel, pencil, graphite, acrylic by Erin Petson.

Petson continues to fuel her passion for her work. "Fashion is constantly changing, so it never loses its appeal," she says. "Fashion illustration is a beautiful craft and it's so wonderful to see so much of it around. I'd love to see it on the front cover of *Vogue* again. It's such a pleasure and honor for me to do what I love for a living, and I'm so grateful to all of the people who have helped me along the way. Here's to me getting the cover of *Vogue.*"

Erin Petson hand-embellished prints.

A travel sketchbook and promotional limited-edition postcard that Erin Petson keeps in her sketchbook.

Lanvin A/W 14 Paris Fashion Week sketch, ink, pastel, pencil, graphite, acrylic by Erin Petson.

Floral Spring Study
A work in progress by Erin Petson.

A sketch from London Fashion Week, backstage at Cristina Sabaiduc by Erin Petson.

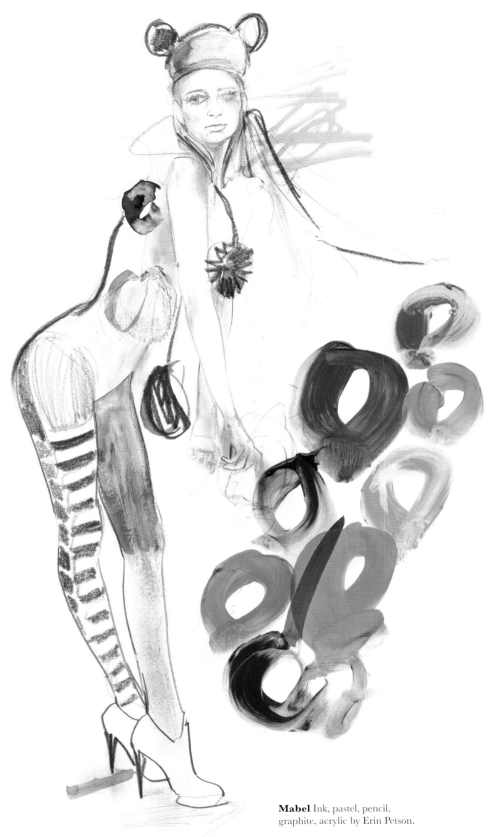

Influences

Although inspired by the works of Paul Verhoeven, Richard Gray, René Gruau, Demetrios Psillos, and the fashion designs of Dior, Chanel, and Victoria Beckham, Petson's technique is all her own. It is delicate, abstract, and ethereal all at the same time.

Good Advice

"Really find your style. It defines you and makes you stand out from the crowd," Petson advises. "Learn the business, learn marketing, intern at an ad agency or a magazine or a fashion house, and get your work published! Draw every day."

Mabel Ink, pastel, pencil, graphite, acrylic by Erin Petson.

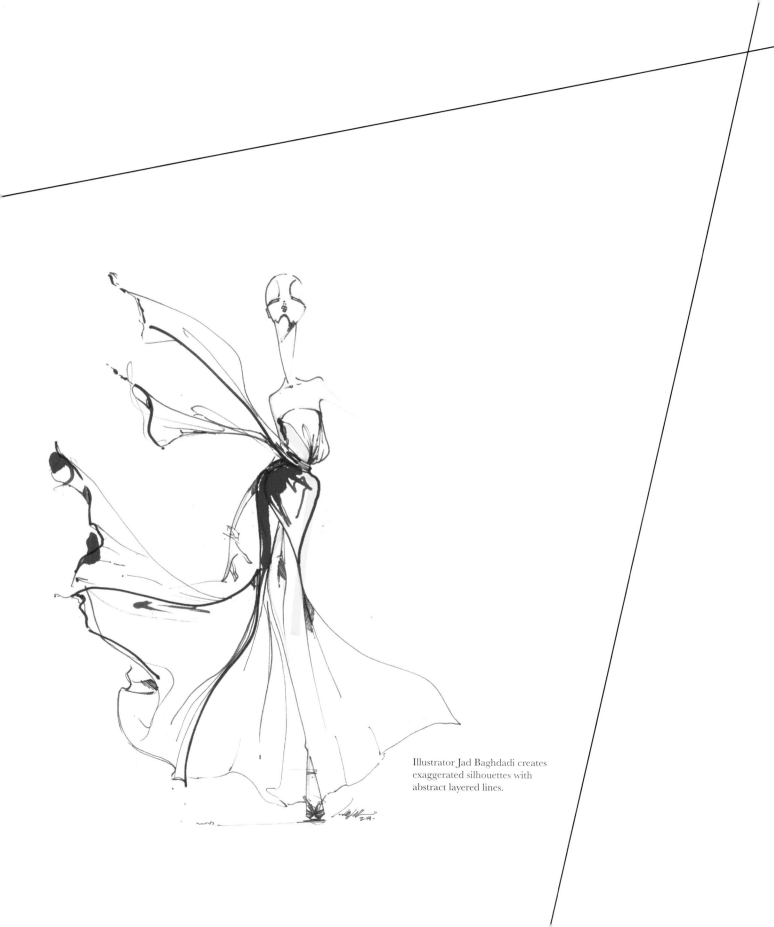

Illustrator Jad Baghdadi creates
exaggerated silhouettes with
abstract layered lines.

CONTRIBUTOR INDEX

GLOSSARY OF TERMS

Aesthetic
The nature of beauty, art, and taste; relating to an artist's taste—what he or she finds beautiful.

Blind contour
A technique in which the artist looks at the paper as little as possible and instead keeps his gaze on the inspiration piece.

Composition
The arrangement or placement of the elements in a drawing.

Editorial illustration
An illustration a magazine or newspaper uses with an article that helps interpret the article's concepts or elements to the reader.

Gouache
An opaque watercolor used by some illustrators.

Illustrator
Graphic design software from Adobe.

Light box
A translucent surface illuminated from below that an artist can use to trace photos, pictures, or past illustrations.

Medium
The substance an illustrator uses to create his work. Examples: ink, watercolor, or paint.

Mixed media
An illustration in which more than one substance or process is used to create the work.

Monochrome

An illustration in one color or shades of one color.

Palette

The range of colors an illustrator chooses for a drawing.

Photorealism

An illustration or painting style that mimics a photograph, using meticulous detail, to render the subject as realistically as possible.

Photoshop

A software application from Adobe for editing photographs and illustrations.

References

Images, text, or photographs an artist may use for inspiration or as a starting point for a drawing.

René Gruau

A renowned fashion illustrator (1909–2004) known as a favorite of the haute couture and luxury fashion worlds, who worked for Christian Dior and Givenchy, among others. His illustrations are in museums and galleries including the Louvre.

Silhouette

The shape or outline or contour of a work.

Visual language

A way of communicating with pictorial elements such as illustrations or photographs rather than words.

She Wore Red "The inspiration was Australian fashion designer Alex Perry. I loved the dress, the color, and movement—it's just so beautiful and was really fun to illustrate," Hankinson explains.

Art by Julie Johnson

Fashion illustration is a direct connection to the creative eye; it inspires and expresses the fluidity of a sketch, the mood of a collection, the beauty of a garment. Illustration elongates the body and the clothing in a uniquely poetic way that cannot be reproduced as effectively in any other medium. It evokes a timelessness designers are always looking to capture.

—**Stefania Amfitheatrof, luxury fashion industry public relations executive**

Lindsey Wixson for Prada Spring 2014,
watercolor by Caroline Andrieu.

ABOUT THE AUTHOR

Somer Tejwani has worked in almost every aspect of the fashion and beauty industry from stylist to fashion journalist, professor to marketing director, writer and editor. Her work has appeared in national magazines, luxury advertising campaigns, catalogues, and in the wardrobes of private clients throughout the country.

Her career in fashion started early as some of her first memories are of spending summers styling the mannequins that graced the window fronts of the neighborhood charity thrift shop. Years later she became a journalist and covered fashion, design, and lifestyle topics for websites and magazines. While working at a magazine, she got her first break as a stylist on a fashion shoot. She was hooked on how the clothing dramatically changed the feeling of each shot and created a story. After that first photo shoot, her career progressed with more fashion shoots, teaching styling and fashion journalism at the university level, and two previously published books on beauty and fashion.

Somer currently lives in southern California with her husband, Sam, and son, Kai. She continues to write for award-winning magazines and develop campaigns for beauty, fashion, and lifestyle brands.

ACKNOWLEDGMENTS

The Art of Fashion Illustration celebrates the talent of some of the world's best artists. Thank you to all of them for sharing their craft, their images, and being so open to sharing their techniques with the readers. There is no such thing as a perfect experience when it comes to writing a book—but the team behind *The Art of Fashion Illustration* made it just as close as you can get. Thank you to the whole family at Quarto Publishing Group, including my project manager Betsy Gammons, who tirelessly got behind this book—without you it wouldn't have seen the light of day. Thank you to Emily Potts for seeing the vision and carrying the torch for this book. Thank you to Ginger Budrick, a gem of an editorial assistant, for helping me organize so many biographies, interviews, and illustrations in one book. Thank you to my husband, Sam, for putting up with the long hours and always giving honest feedback about my writing. Last, but certainly not least, thank you to my son, Kai, for being born just as I turned in my final draft of this manuscript … good timing!

Fashion illustration allows the design fantasy to come to life. It is a road map to new ideas; and one sketch can often spiral, cultivating a unique emotional connection, influencing an entire collection.

—Misha Nonoo of Nonoo New York and 2013 CFDA/*Vogue* Fashion Fund Finalist

SKETCH YOUR OWN FASHIONS

Now Get Sketching!

You've just discovered what makes some of the world's top fashion illustrators unique. Now you can try out the techniques they've described here to create your own works of art using the fashion silhouettes printed on the high-quality, uncoated drawing paper provided. They are perforated for easy removal. You might start with Danny Robert's blind contour style, in which you place your pen on the paper and look only at the subject, drawing blindly. As artist Sarah Beetson said, this technique "can be totally haphazard with moments of clarity, a mess of abstract lines with a perfect hand or eye within it"—so if the technique doesn't give you the intended result, don't be afraid to mix and match it with other techniques until you find a style that is truly your own.

Perhaps you'll be inspired by Silja Götz to play with different materials to create a collage within a traditional ink silhouette drawing, or by artist Yaeko Abe who draws in ink pen before adding color with markers, all while staying loose and spontaneous. Once you've developed a sketch you're happy with, keep it in your personal archive like artist Lovisa Burfitt, who used to throw away her finished sketches, but now keeps the ones she's happy with to use as inspiration for future drawings.

Each of the artists in this book has one thing in common: They worked hard to achieve their success; it didn't happen overnight. Practice and perfect your style and make it your own, because there is nothing more important than the individual point of view an artist brings to a project.

For me illustration is a way of exploring details. Since my collections begin with fabric—the texture, pattern, color, and opulence—illustration gets my ideas and silhouettes onto paper; fine-tuning the details and discovering new ones from the slip of the hand.

—Erica Tanov, fashion designer

Sketches are the soul of a collection. It's that special magical moment in the beginning when your pen hits the paper and a small idea unravels into a big dream or a beautiful story.

—Danielle Goodman, luxury fashion industry public relations executive

An idea is just a dream when trapped in your head, but it becomes a reality when you put it down on paper.

—Leslie S. Christen, stylist and fashion editor

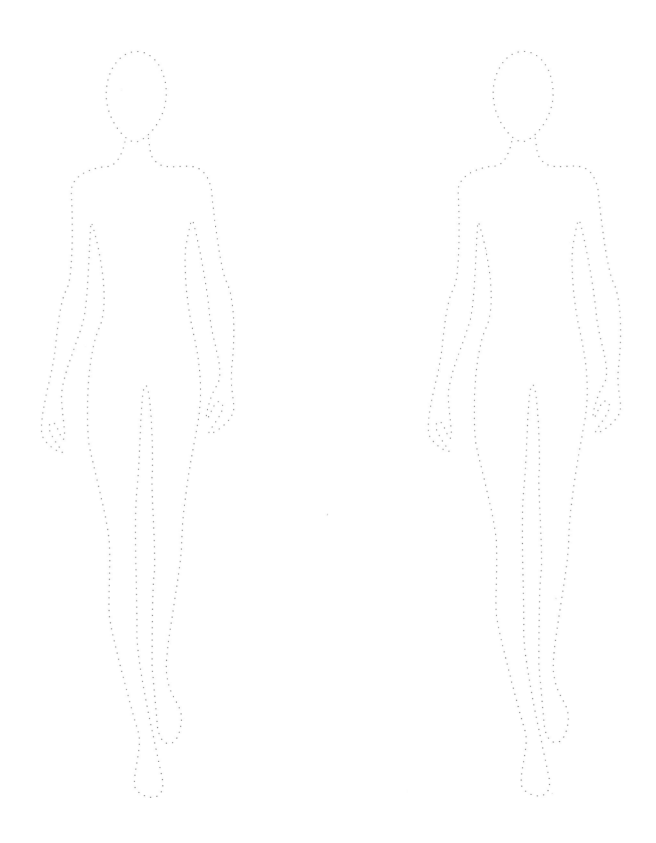

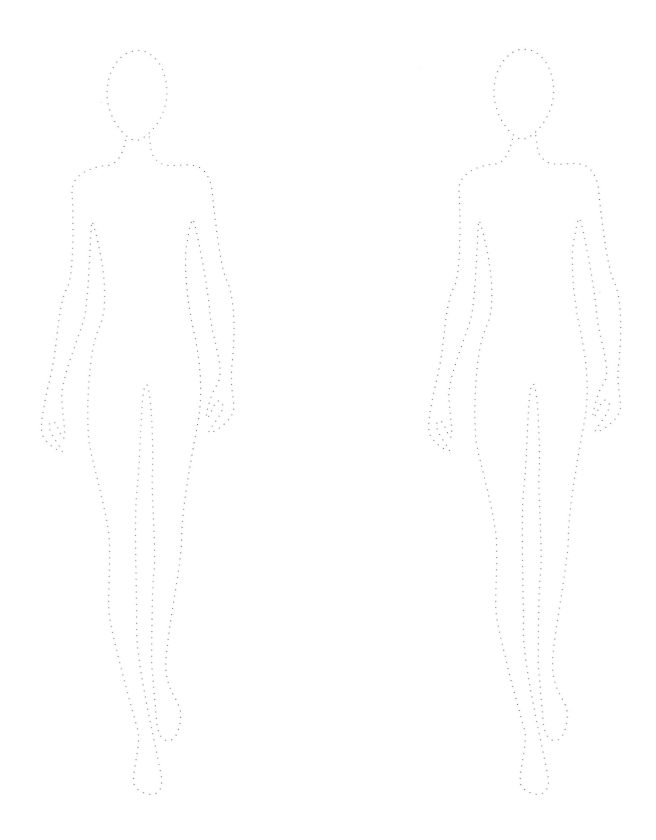

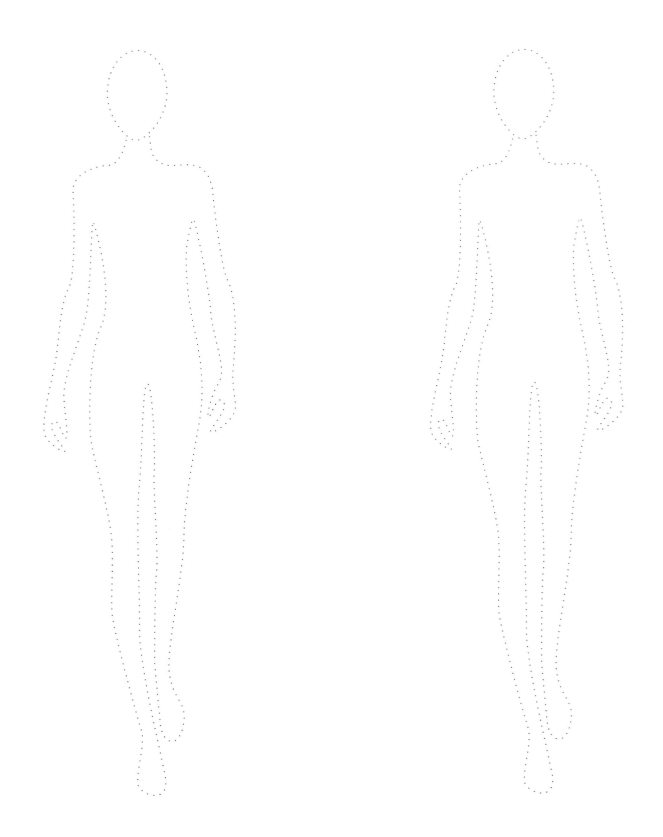

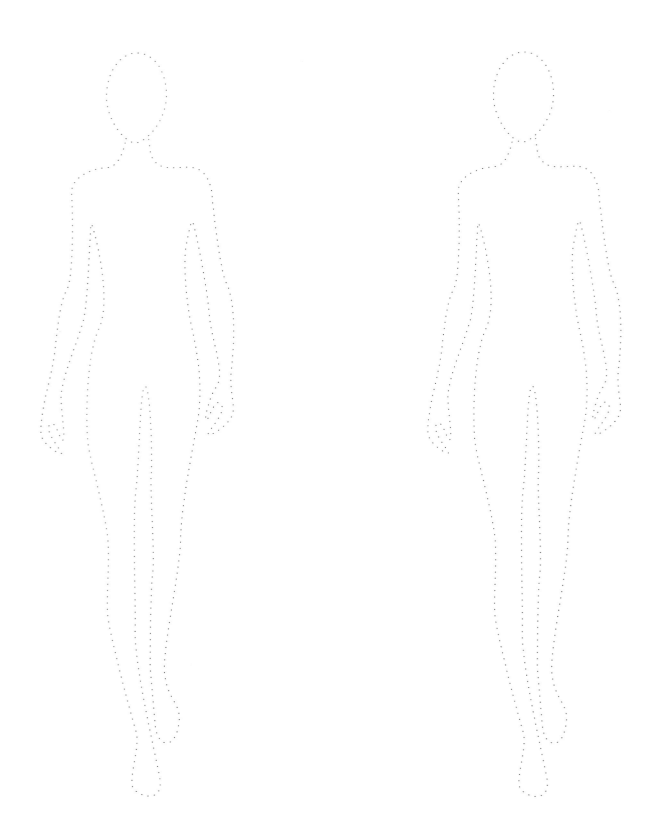

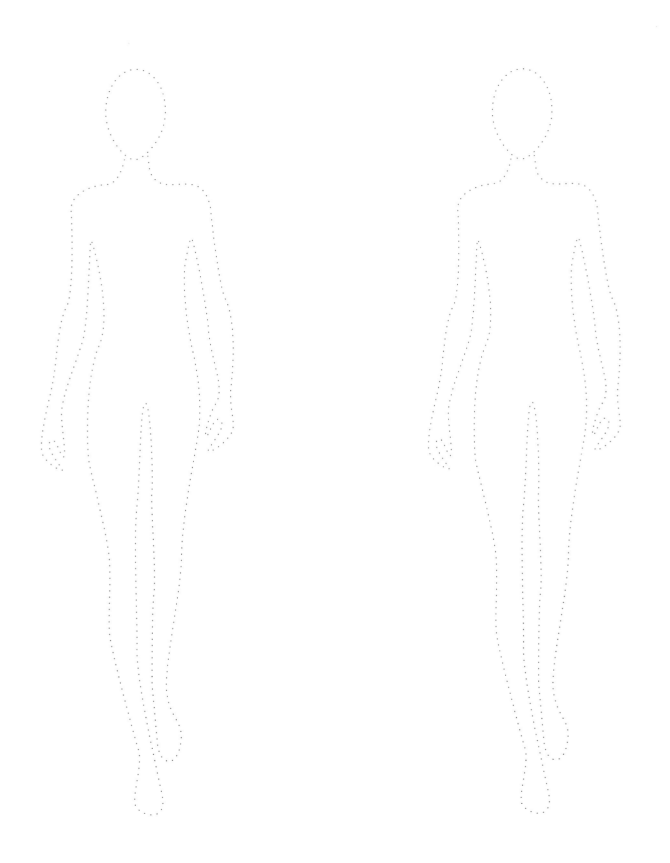

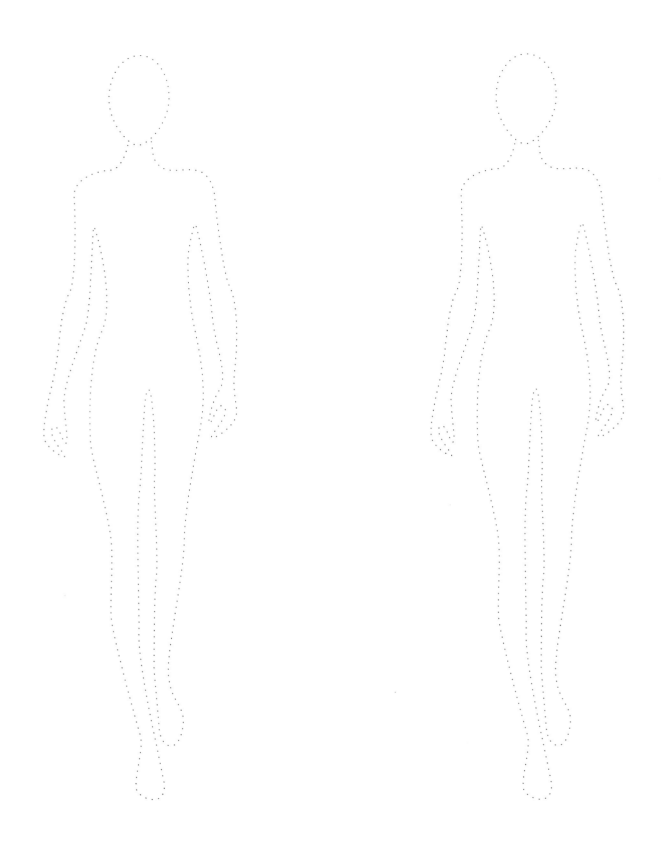

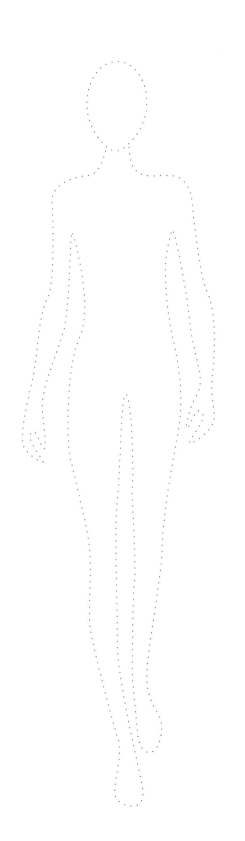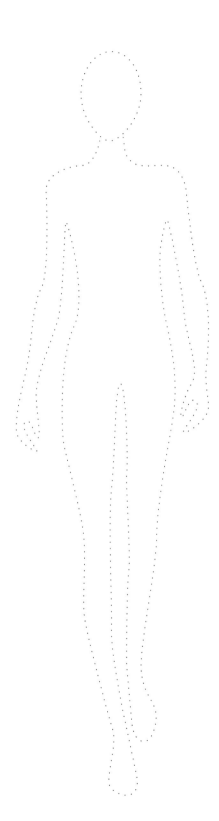

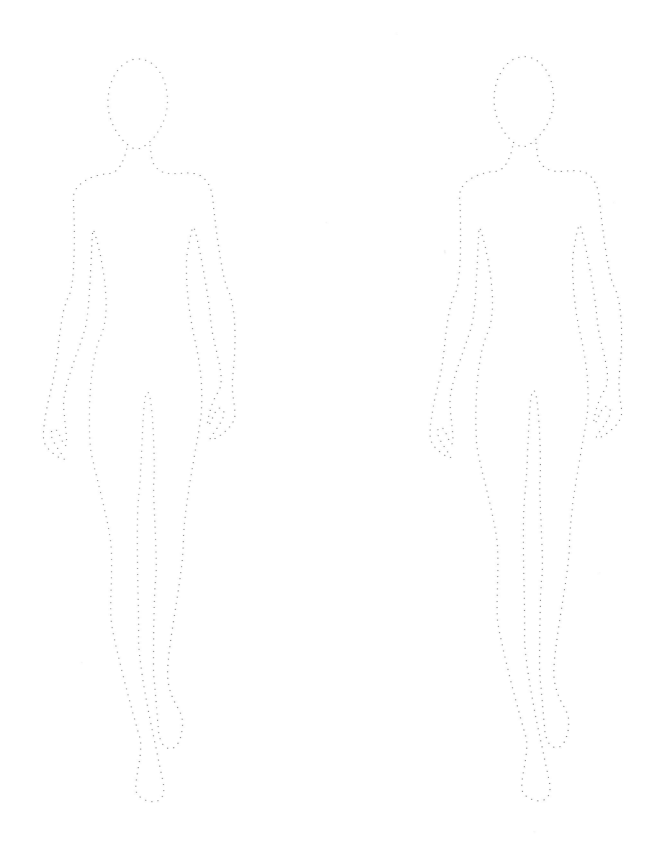

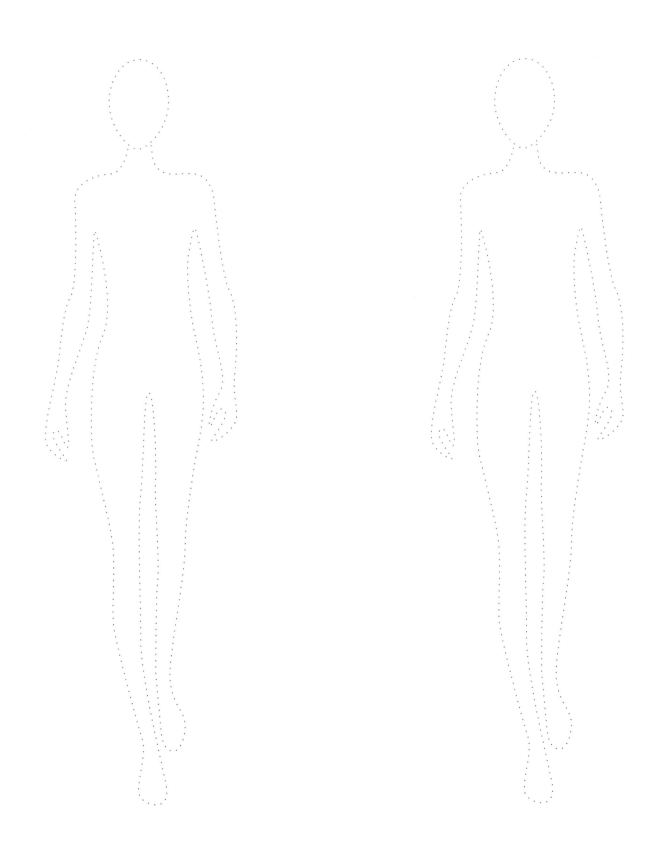

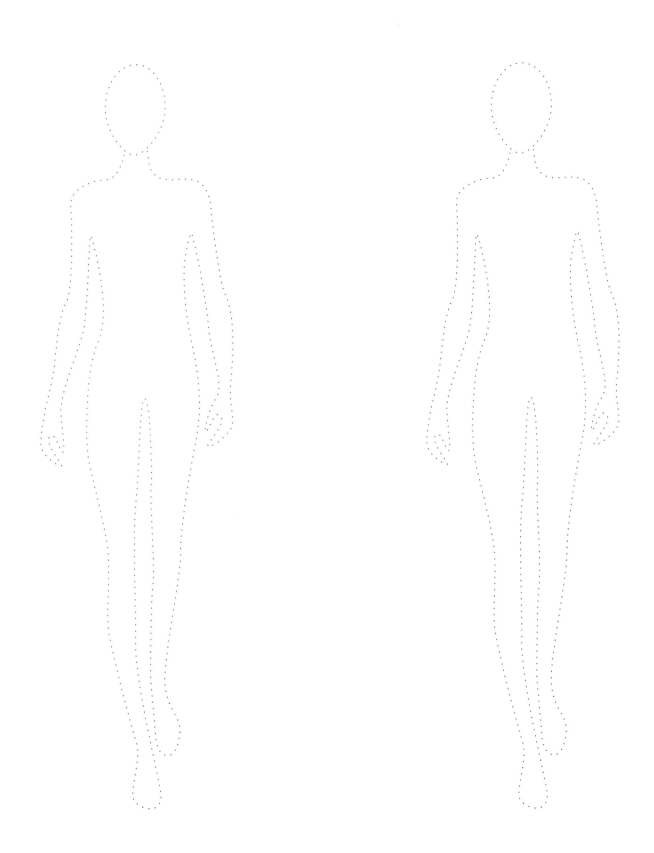

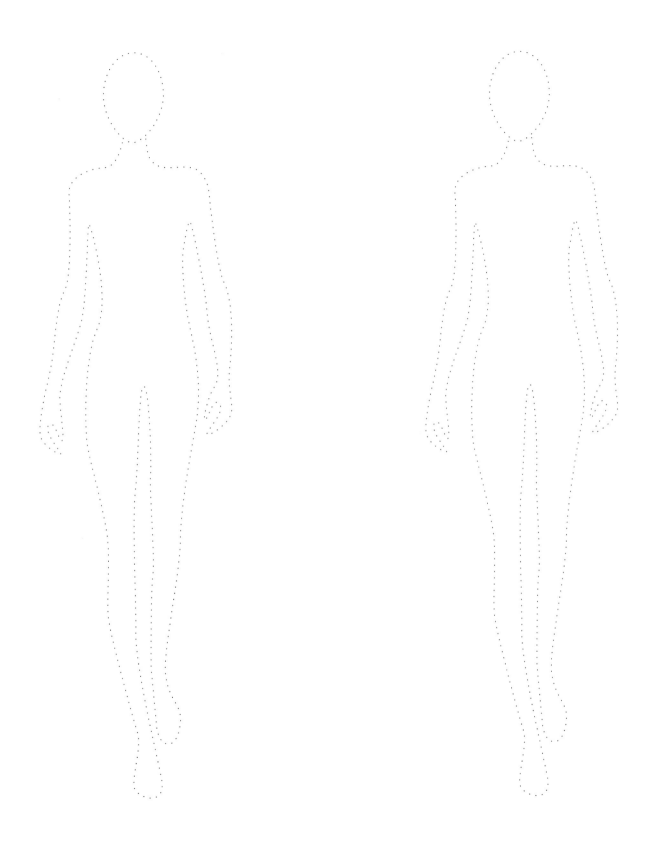

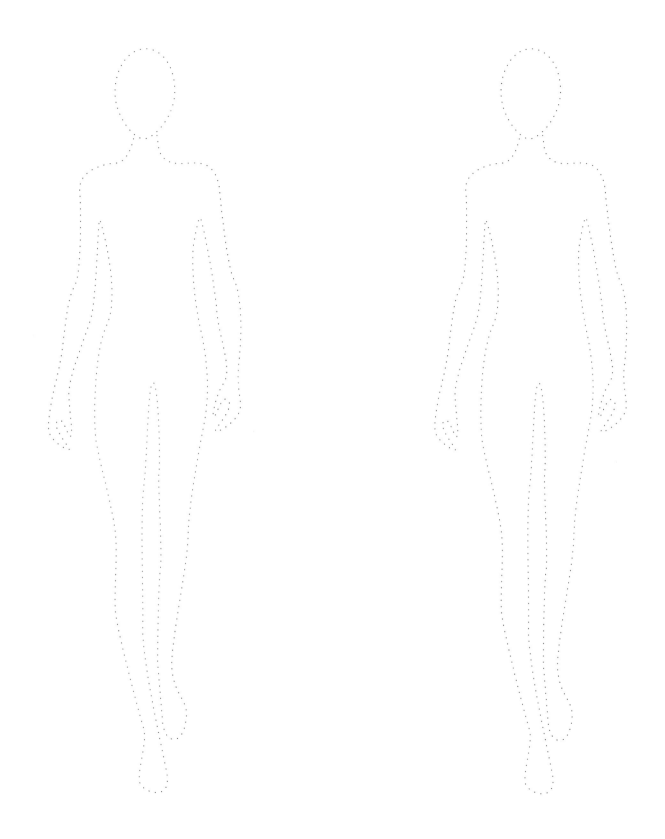

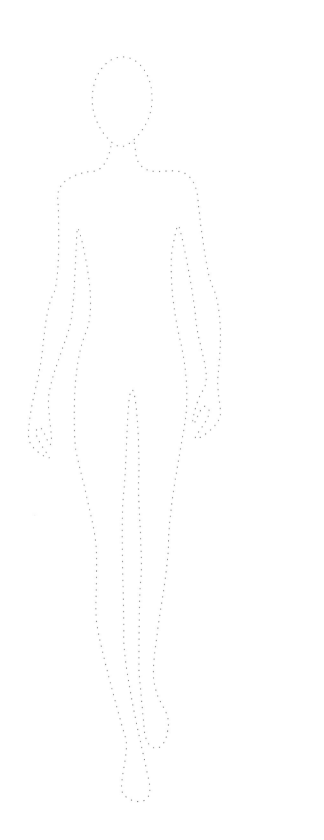
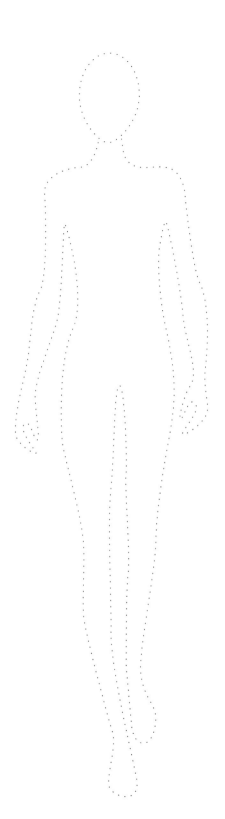

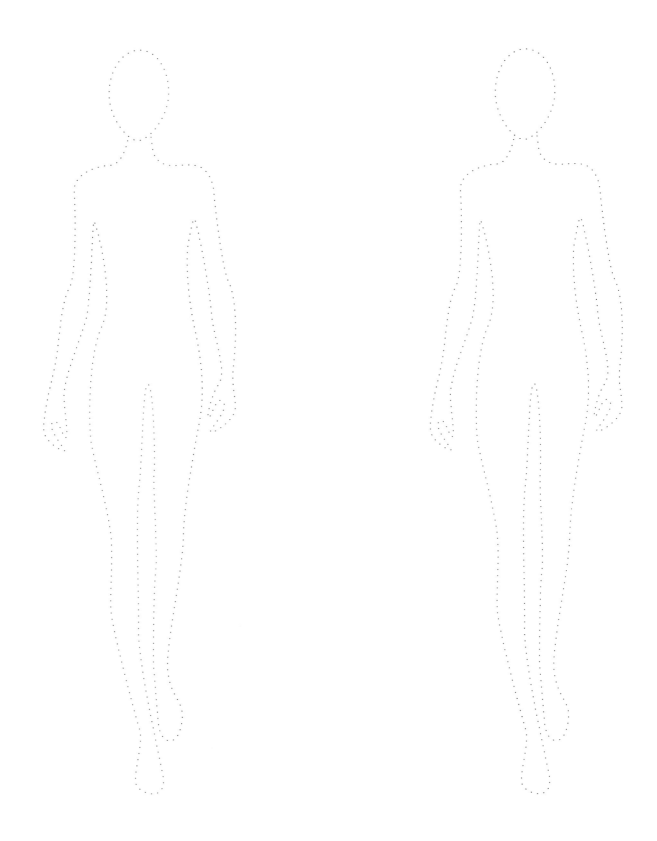

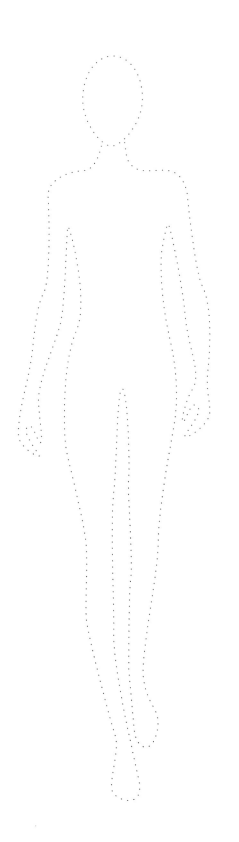

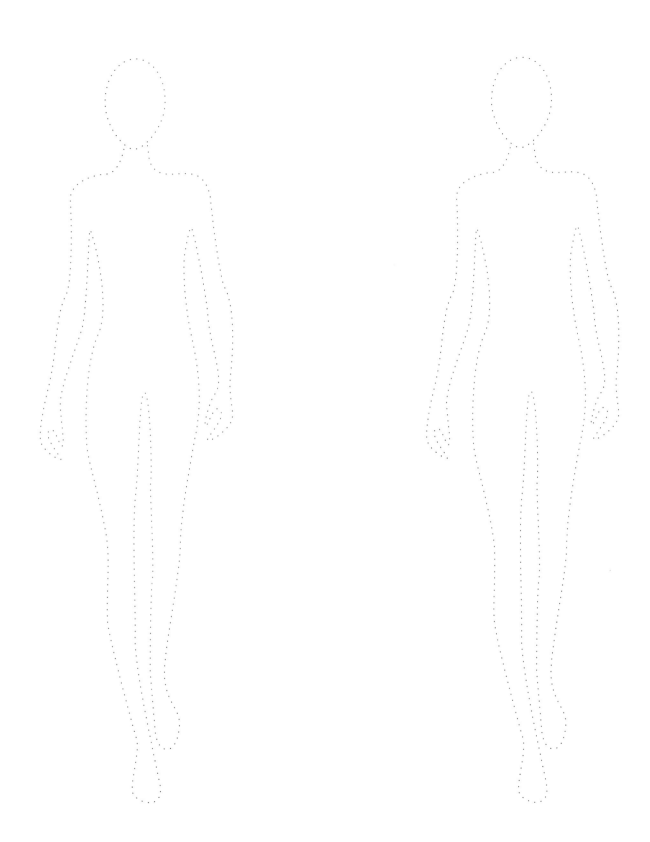

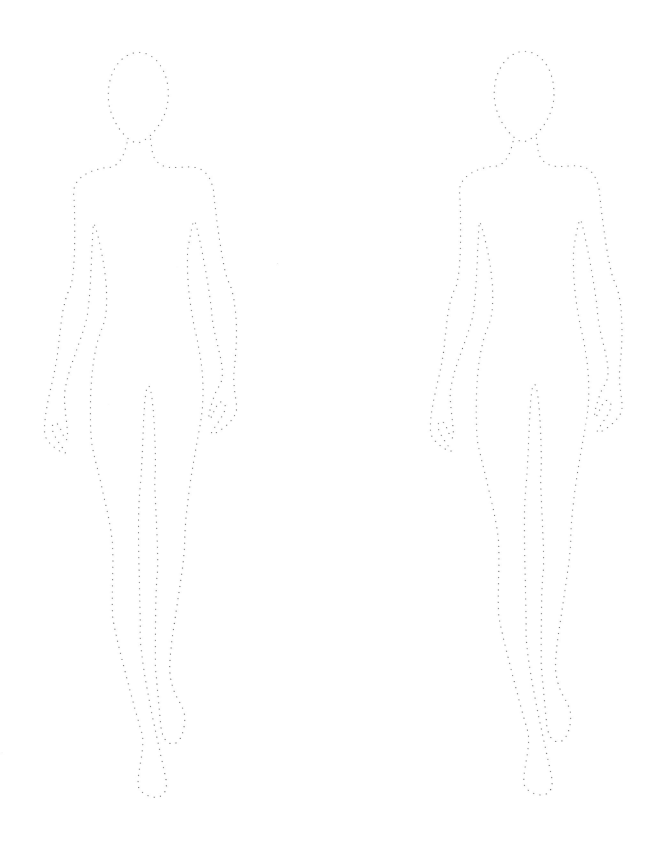

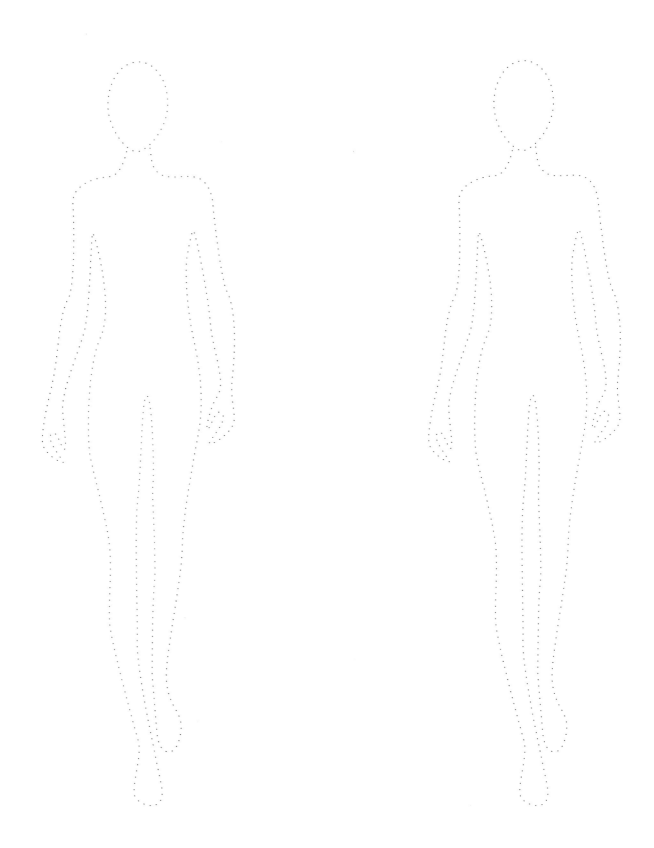

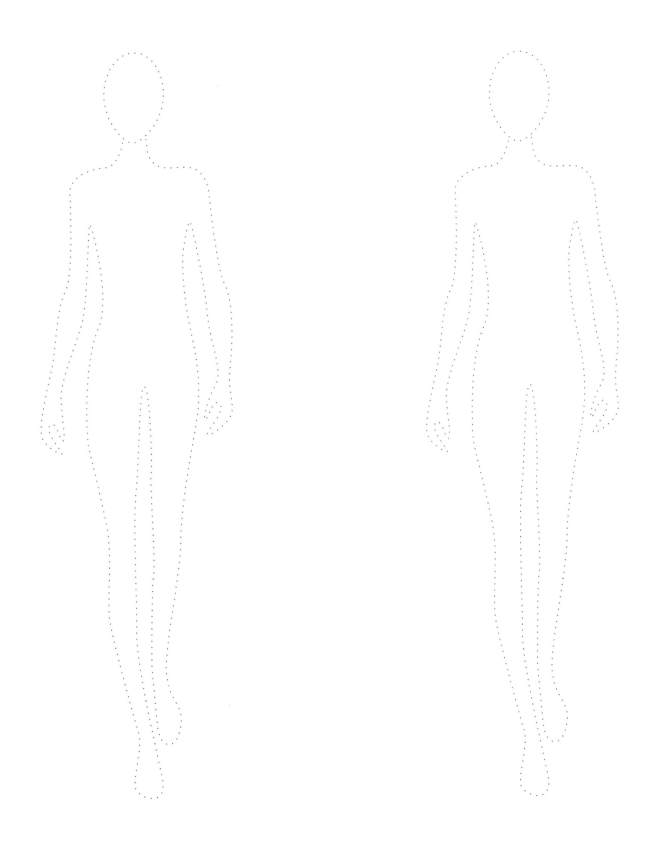

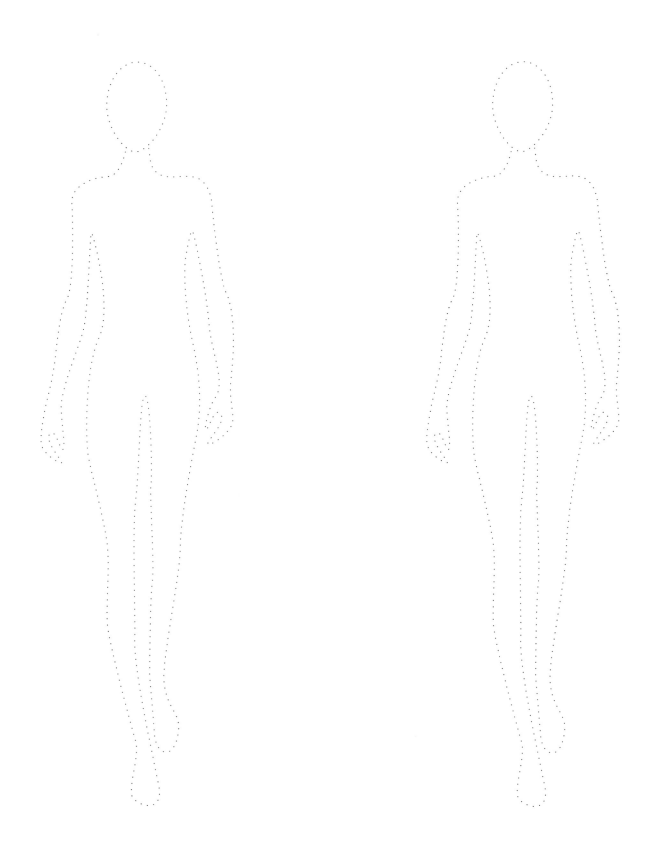

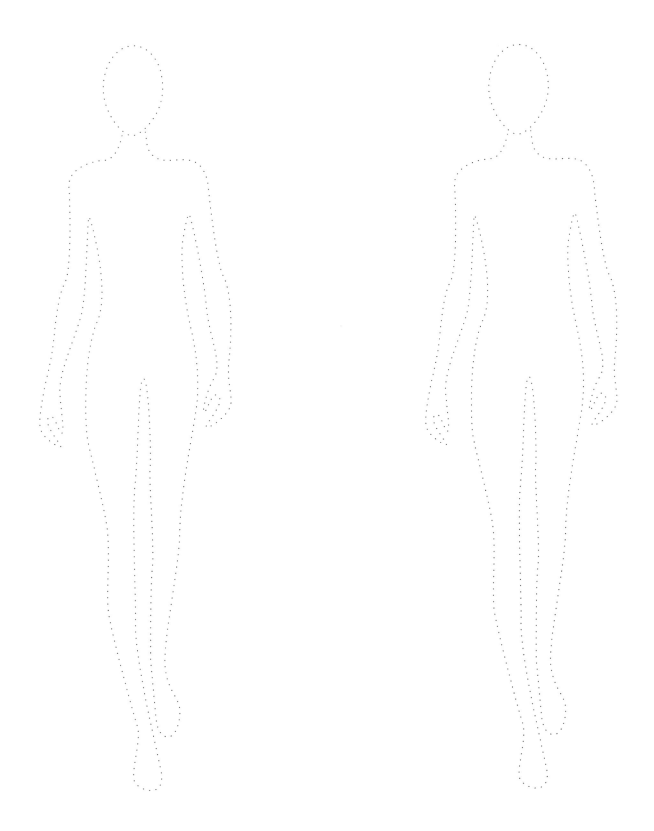

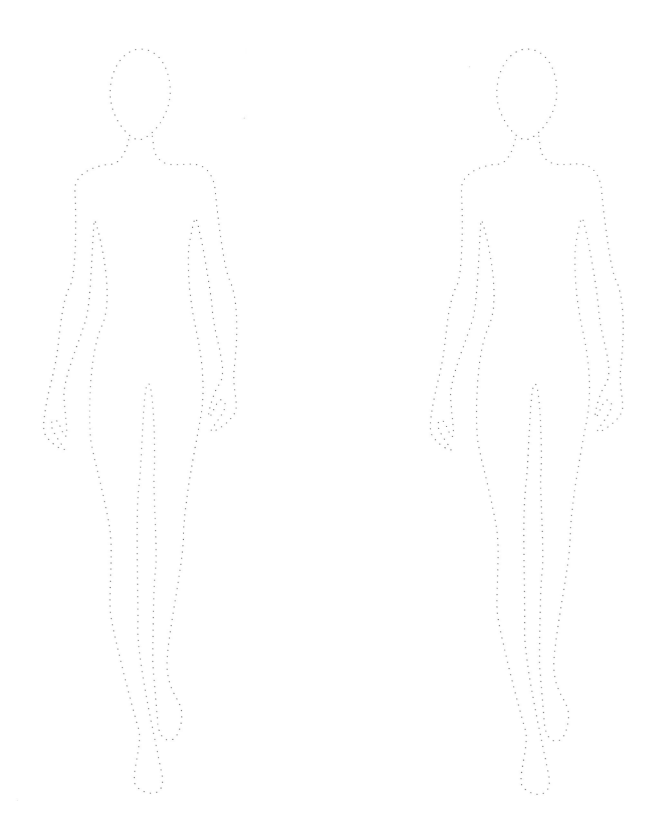

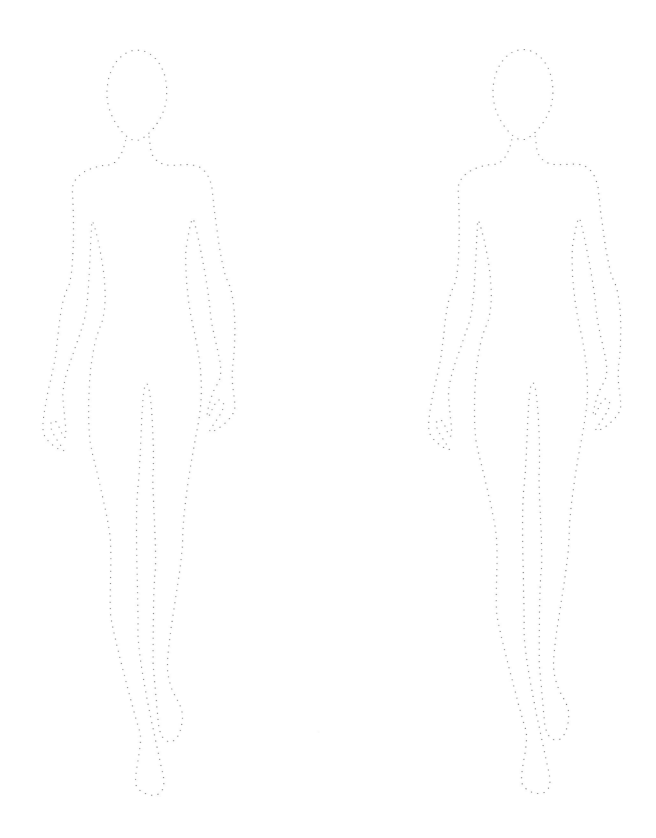

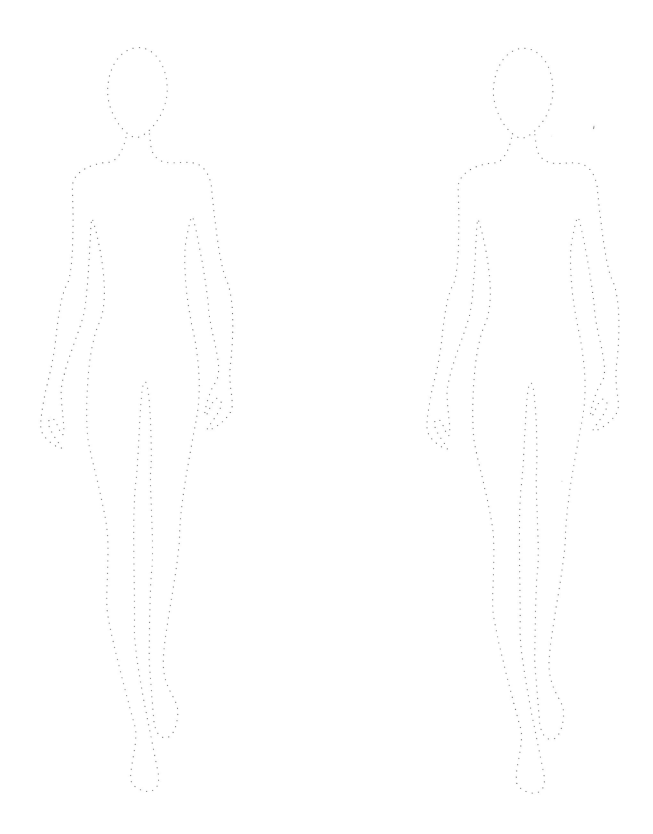

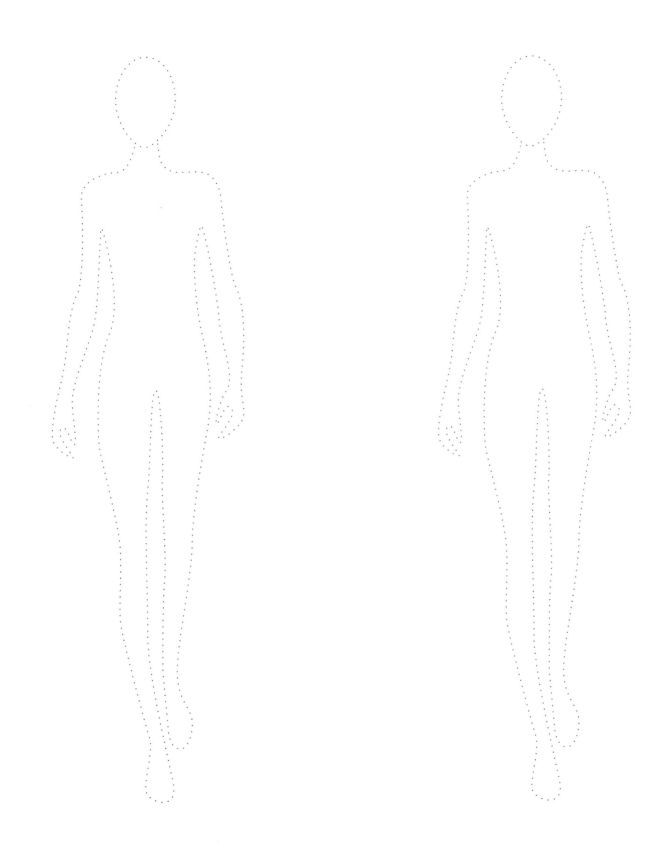

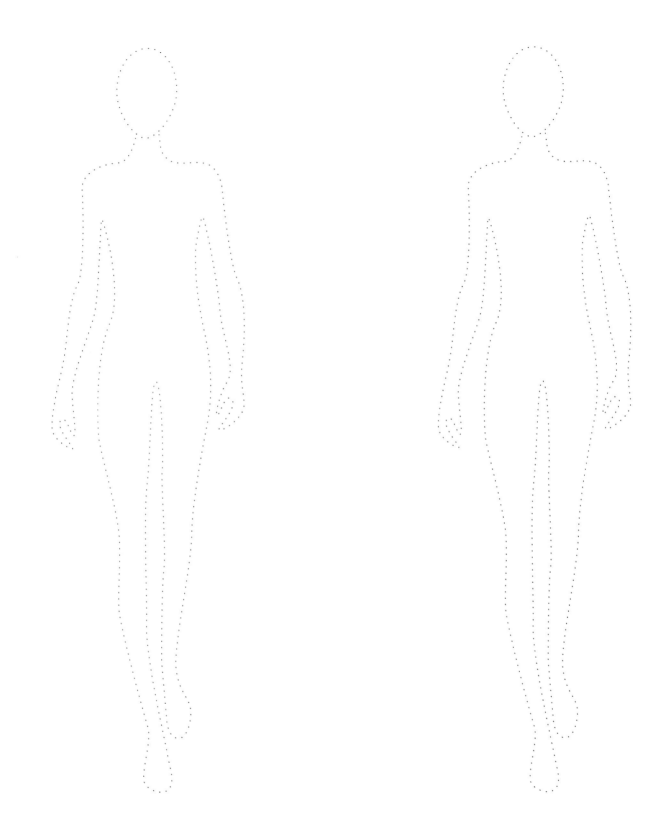

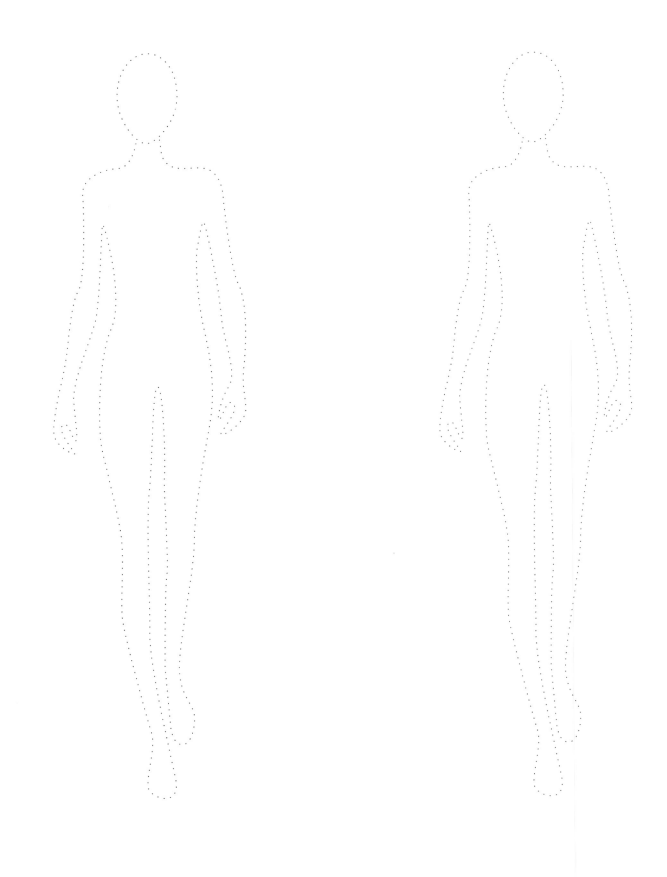

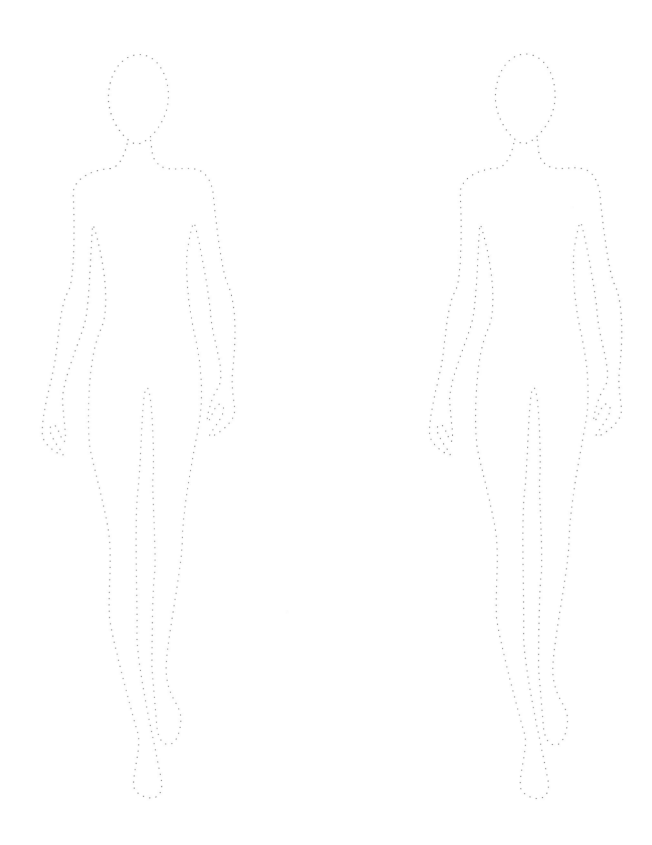

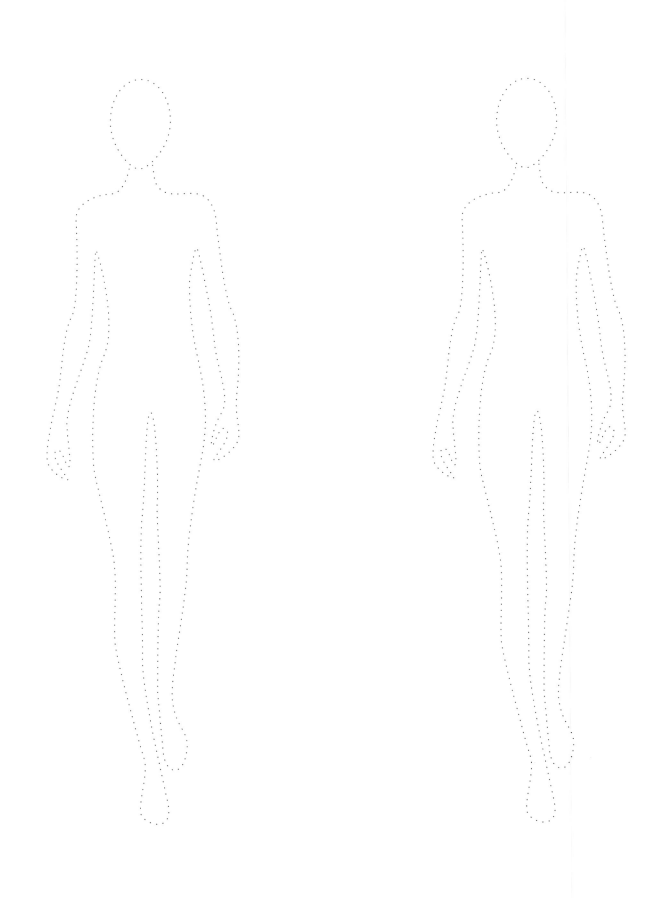

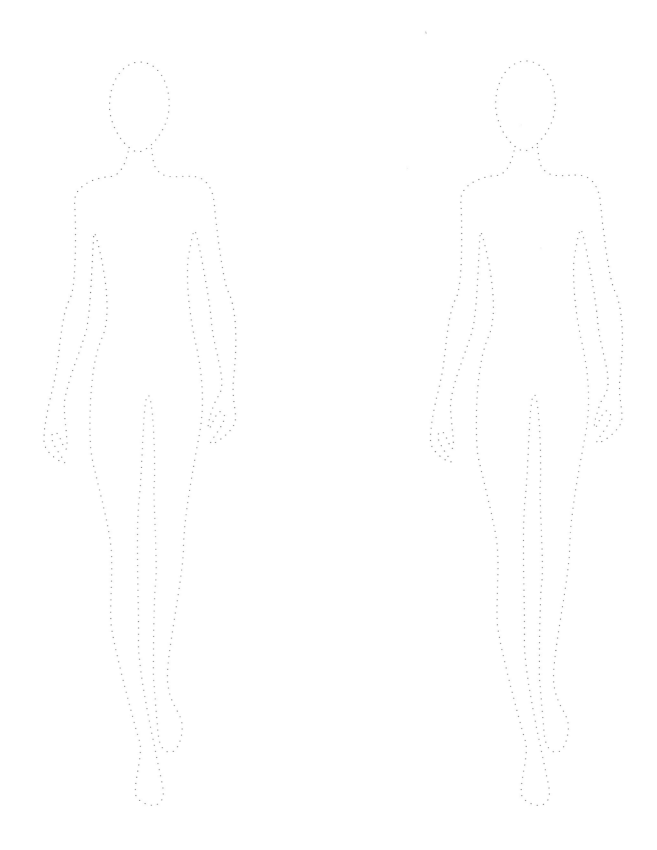

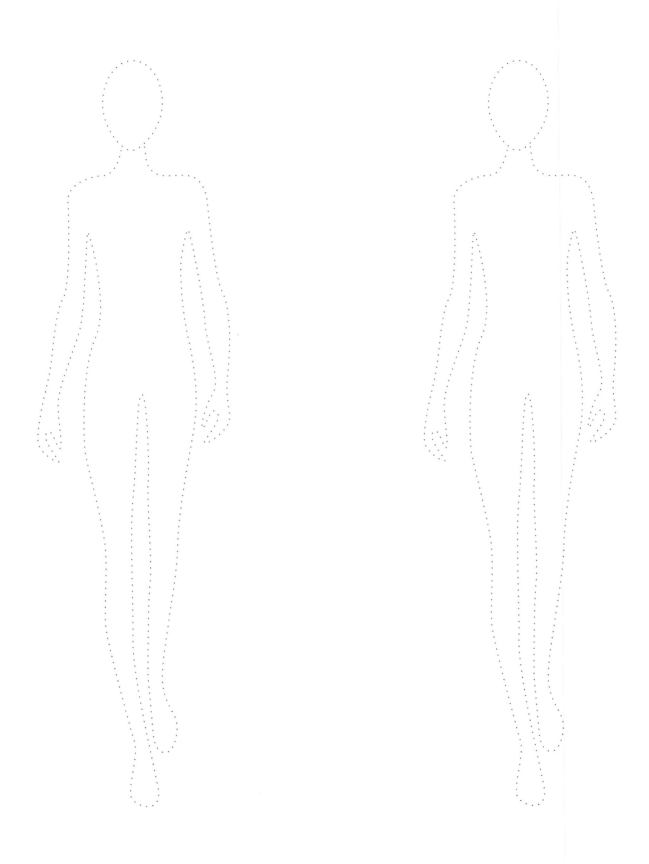

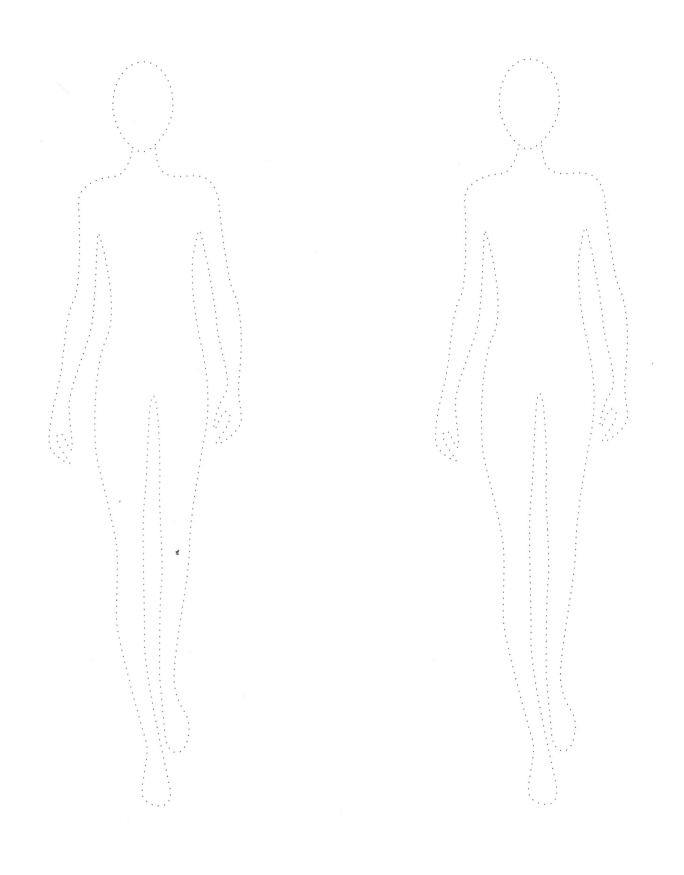